D0274324

COUNTRY WALKS

AROUND

BATH

Tim Mowl has written several books about Bath, most notably the 1988 biography of the architect John Wood, which established the theory that the creation of the Georgian city was influenced by Druidic stone circles and Freemasonic ritual. He co-wrote with Adam Fergusson, *The Sack of Bath and After*, a re-issue of the devastating analysis of the destruction of artisan areas of the city with his update on planning since the 1970s. In the mid-1980s he was Architectural Adviser to the Bath Preservation Trust and following that wrote a provocative weekly column on architecture for the *Bath Evening Chronicle*. In 1996 he wrote a study of the 18th-century Gothick fancier, Horace Walpole, and his latest biography, published in June 1998, is on William Beckford, builder of the legendary Fonthill Abbey near Salisbury and the Lansdown Tower in Bath. He is married with one son and lives in Bristol.

Worcester Lodge, Badminton Estate

Tim Mowl's
COUNTRY WALKS
AROUND
BATH

with illustrations by Alan and Dennis Summers

Millstream Books

for Brian
and with thanks to Sarah
for reading maps and sampling pub food for the revised edition

Millstream Books
18 The Tyning
Bath BA2 6AL

First edition 1986
Second, revised edition 1989
Reprinted with corrections 1991
Third, revised and reset edition 1998

Set in Times New Roman and printed in Great Britain by
The Matthews Wright Press, Chard, Somerset

© Tim Mowl 1986, 1989 and 1998

ISBN 0948975164

All rights reserved. No part of this publication may be
reproduced, stored in a retrieval system, or transmitted, in any
form or by any means, electronic, mechanical, photocopying,
recording or otherwise, without the prior permission of
Millstream Books.

Contents

The valley of the Cam Brook at Combe Hay

Introduction

Shall we be honest about it? There is perhaps one other part of Europe that is in the same class for civilised walking as the hills around Bath. It is the Dordogne. It has the same richly-sculpted river valleys, the same golden stone. For castles it scores heavily, on churches and farmhouses the two regions tie. On just one vital comparison Bath is way ahead: the Dordogne has nothing like the network of field paths that gives every Mendip and Cotswold walk so many variants, such a delightful sense of pioneering without peril. Be warned: if you use this book you will constantly be tempted by other stiles, other lanes and other footbridges. The permutations are endless and so are the rewards. This region has been blessed by its history and its geology. As a result you will have slow walking with a village, farmstead, prehistoric stone or brambled industrial relic turning up literally every few yards to delay you.

Because of this factor, the longest of these walks, round ducal Badminton, is a mere ten miles and some are only two or three. They are graded:

A. 6 to 10 miles,   a full afternoon or morning walk, suitable for a picnic break.
B. 3 to 6 miles,   a modest leg-stretcher between meals.
C. 2 to 3 miles,   a mini-tramp with lots to occupy your eyes and perhaps a note or sketch book.

You will have your favourite footwear, but these walks were all tested in ordinary sensible shoes. In wet weather you may prefer wellies or walking boots, and I have indicated in the text those parts which may sometimes be muddy.

Since conservation and criticism of new building are now part of our daily lives, it should be said in fairness that the landowners and local authorities around Bath deserve some praise. Most hedgerows survive, barbed wire blockage of ways is rare. While nothing can equal the two-step stiles on the rights of way across Bath Spa University College's Newton Park estate, most paths have either a stile or a signpost at their outset. If the markers tend to falter a few fields later, then that is half the pleasure of a walk. No one wants a fenced and regulated route like the Cotswold Way up Kelston Round Hill to become standard. People, not institutions, keep footpaths alive.

The walk descriptions may seem to stress architecture at the expense of flora and fauna. That is not because the flowers and animals are less rich, just that they are more vulnerable. Make your own discoveries.

Opinions on architecture old and new are highly subjective, but the bias of the writing is towards a living, evolving countryside rather than a postcard prettiness. A hamlet like Inglesbatch with its skyline of metal silos may not be everyone's ideal, but its farms are working units and its lanes are pashed an honest brown with cow hooves and cow muck. Restoration can be too finicky. Test your opinions against mine. You may like the pickled gentility of Wellow or the hardworking new estates at Marshfield. I don't. Mells village is a delight, but there is modern housing in Combe Hay finer than much of the average 17th-century vernacular.

It is hard to write about buildings without some technical terms, but I hope I have explained these when they occur in the text.

I saw no bulls and all my dogs were friendly when I first produced these walks in 1986. When revising the book in the spring of 1998 I noticed more cats and two goats at Dunkerton. Paths are far better signed now and farmers seem more responsible in their stewardship of rights of way. But what alarmed me was to see just how many textured cottages of the first edition had been sanitised and visually wrecked by the insertion of replacement plastic windows. 'Neighbourhood

Watch' signs proliferate and too many churches are locked. Most depressing of all, the easy-going social life of some villages has been permanently damaged by the closure of their local pubs. If we are not careful we will all end up in a cocoon of television and our own company. If these walks get people out into the country to enjoy the last dregs of our fast disappearing heritage, and encourage them to swap anecdotes with passers-by about lost paths and 'things to look out for' not yet spotted, then they will have served their purpose.

Tim Mowl, Bristol, 1998

Publisher's Note

Maps. The maps for each walk are drawn to a scale of 1:30,000 (approximately 2 inches to 1 mile) except for Walks 12 – Marshfield – at 1:10,000 (approximately 6 inches to 1 mile) and 13 – Badminton – at 1:50,000 (approximately 1¹/₄ inches to 1 mile). Any significant features are included, whether necessary for establishing the line of the walk, or relevant for enhancing the enjoyment of the walk.

Rights of Way. All rights of way have been followed as far as possible according to the line shown on Ordnance Survey 1:25,000 maps. In some cases, where a right of way has been shown as crossing a field which is now ploughed or sown, the path has been altered to go round the edge of the field. All routes were checked in the spring of 1998, but if any path is subsequently found to meet such an obstacle, I suggest that you make your own detour, with reference to the appropriate Ordnance Survey map. Walkers and farmers have to coexist amicably if our countryside is to be preserved, and it is only common courtesy for the walker to respect the work of the farmer.

Opening Times. The times given were correct in the spring of 1998, but are always liable to change in the future.

Buses. We have given the bus routes applicable in the spring of 1998. First Badgerline operates all the services mentioned except those for Walks 10 and 12. Information about services available for these latter are given on pages 67 and 81. As routes and numbers may change, it is advisable to check with the Bus Company before departure, and if you plan more than one walk in a week, you may well benefit from various special fare offers. The telephone number of Badgerline is 01225 464446.

The Woods of Bath
on their home ground

Length: For motorists: 5 miles/Grade B
             By bus: 6 miles/Grade B

Map: O.S. Explorer 155 (Bristol & Bath)

Theme: Three villages and a lofty hill fort on the wide-open, south-facing valleys above Bath; a walk that links together the home, the churches and prehistoric inspiration of the family which created Georgian Bath.

Transport: By car – take the A4 London road out of Bath and turn left at Batheaston for Northend. Go past the church and park opposite Eagle House (ST 779684).
By bus – catch the frequent Nos.13 or 13B to Batheaston and walk from the main road to Eagle House. On Mondays, Wednesdays and Fridays (excluding Bank Holidays) No.781 will take you to Eagle House but you will have to return from Batheaston.

Things to look out for:
1   An eagle perched on a parapet
2   The hill where Bladud practised his Druidic 'Inchantments'
3   A village that turns its back on the street
4   A rare Charles I Coat of Arms
5   John Wood of Bath's last resting place
6   A church that starts out Gothick and ends up Classical
7   The originator of Puget Sound, Seattle

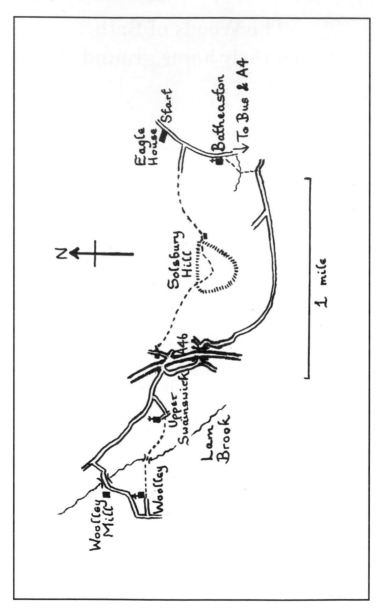

Itinerary

We begin at the house where the younger John Wood lived from 1773 until his death in 1781. The modest early 18th-century building was given a rich roadside front with a niche and stone eagle above in 1729, and a new doorcase – both in a fruiter classicism than the regular Palladian façades the Woods were to impose upon Bath.

Walk down the village street towards the main road and turn right up Seven Acres Lane. At the top of the lane go into the field by the footpath sign. Your path to Solsbury Hill Camp crosses three stiles with the hedges on your right. All the time you are climbing steeply with the camp above you to the left and sweeping views over St Catherine's valley to the ruins of The Rocks (Walk 11). Cross the fourth field diagonally to a stile by a house and make directly for the upper ramparts. Here on Solsbury Hill, John Wood the Elder, in his book on Bath, describes how the legendary King Bladud cast his incantatory magic spells and in a state of trance fell to his death.

Walk across the top of the camp and down the outer ditch to the right and make for a footpath sign where three paths meet. Take the path down through the hedge over a stile. Keep to the edge of the field with the ground falling dramatically below to your right into Chilcombe Bottom and walk towards the house with the cypress trees. As you reach the house, follow the lane left, down to the lorry-ridden A46 dual carriageway. This is the new Swainswick and Batheaston by-pass and it has made things worse, for walkers at least. So cross carefully to the slip-road which will lead you into Upper Swainswick.

Here the houses on the left turn their best faces to the splendid view over to Lansdown, but on the right is Smallman's of about 1720 with chamfered mullions, a bull's eye window and a roof of beautifully graded stone slates. Fork left and go down to the church noting the footpath at the bottom corner which you will follow shortly.

St Mary's is usually open and an old photograph just inside the church shows how little it has been altered since John Wood was buried here; even the fine curvilinear tracery in the nave has survived 19th-century restoration. The nave and aisle still have their textured whitewash and there is a beautiful Victorian pulpit with Connemara marble shafts, oddly sited on the wrong side of the nave. There are fascinating architectural problems posed by the tower arch with its mediaeval faces and what looks to be a later, classical winged angel. And don't miss the sturdy Arts and Crafts oak chair in the sanctuary.

Wood's black slate memorial slab with its elegantly austere inscription – JOANNIS WOOD/ARMIGERI/SEPULCHRUM – is set in the floor just behind the organ. His actual remains are in a vault just outside the church wall on the north side. He was never a parishioner of Swainswick, but wanted to be buried on the spot where his hero, Bladud, had crashed to his death. Wood believed he was recreating the sun and moon temples of Bladud's lost Druidic Bath when he designed the King's Circus and projected the Royal Crescent. As you go out of the south door look at the rare Charles I coat of arms, quartered with France and dated 1647. In that year the King had lost the Civil War and was a prisoner of the Commonwealth so this must have been a very loyal little parish. Before you leave the churchyard walk round to see the Manor House and its barn close up against the north wall.

Take the footpath (the right of way goes through the garden) diagonally right, down the valley, and make for the cupola of Woolley church which is just visible across the valley among a group of ilexes planted around it. Your path will first cross two stiles and then the Woolley Brook by a metal bridge. The stile at the churchyard wall is guarded by an angular new house in reconstructed stone which sets the pattern for the rest of the village, but take in the church first.

The younger John Wood built it in 1761 for the local patron, Elizabeth Parkin. Perhaps because there had been a mediaeval church on the site, Wood tried his hand at the new Gothick fashion for the box-like nave windows with their Y-tracery and then gave up, adding a jaunty classical cupola. If the church is open go inside to see how inept Wood was at handling spaces. The pew ends have beautifully-carved floral finials, there are

Eagle House, Batheaston

hatchments and atmospheric oil lamps, now converted to electricity. In the churchyard is a 19th-century Gothic tomb with cast iron inscription panels and the Egyptian-style memorial to Admiral Puget who gave his name to Puget Sound in Seattle.

All the houses in the lane up from the church gate have been drastically 'improved' by commuterisation but look out for ammonites set next to plastic windows. The most ingenious restoration is Willege which has a plastic-framed, Quality Street-style oriel window. Walk briskly, turn right at the top by the pump and follow the lane as it lurches headlong downhill past the back of Manor Farm – there, at least, old textures remain. In the valley by the brook to your left is a tall gaunt house which was standing empty when the first edition of this book appeared. Happily it is now Mill Farm, restored with a rustic ochre wash to the walls and vibrant blue sash windows. All it needs is a coat of diluted manure sprayed over the roof to encourage lichen to add colour and texture to the shiny new clay pantiles. This was part of the Woolley Powder Mill complex owned by the Parkin family which manufactured gunpowder for the merchant ships setting out from Bristol in the 18th century. In the wall of the cottage by the road below the complex is the huge socket for the mill wheel.

Turn right at the next junction, fork left past the best front of Swainswick Manor House and retrace your steps through the village to the A46. Follow the signpost to Bath on the old road until you come to the bridge and turn left under the dual carriageway. Then turn right up the single-track road. Follow this lane around the hill camp down towards Batheaston. As the first houses appear take the stile and path left over the fields to the church. Turn left onto the main street and before you reach your car, the Northend pub is worth a stop for wholesome food and a handy beer garden.

Briefly round Biddestone
and the valley of the By Brook

Length: For motorists: 4 (or 6) miles/Grade B
                 By bus: 7 (or 9) miles/Grade A

Maps: O.S. Explorer 156 (Chippenham & Bradford-on-Avon)
             N.B. this is due to be published in 1998. Until then,
             use Pathfinder 1168 (Chippenham & Castle Combe).

Theme: Though only a short walk, perhaps for after lunch,
             this links an almost too picturesque village in level
             North Wiltshire with the watery pleasures of old
             sluices in a deep, wooded valley which is still
             gently industrial. It can be extended by another 2
             miles if you feel energetic.

Transport: By car – take the A4 London road as far as Corsham,
             bear left to avoid the town centre, then take the
             second turning left to Biddestone. Park on one of
             the little roads by the duck pond (ST 864735).
             By bus – not so easy, though there is a frequent
             service to Chippenham (Nos. X32, X34 & 231)
             which will drop you at the Biddestone turning,
             $1^1/_2$ miles from the village.

Things to look out for:
1 A mill wheel without a mill
2 Gazebos
3 The rock formations that made all the golden roof tiles
   you've been seeing
4 A pool where Rupert Brooke might have wanted to swim
5 Benefaction boards
6 One of the earliest bell-turrets in England
7 A restored farmhouse fit for William Morris

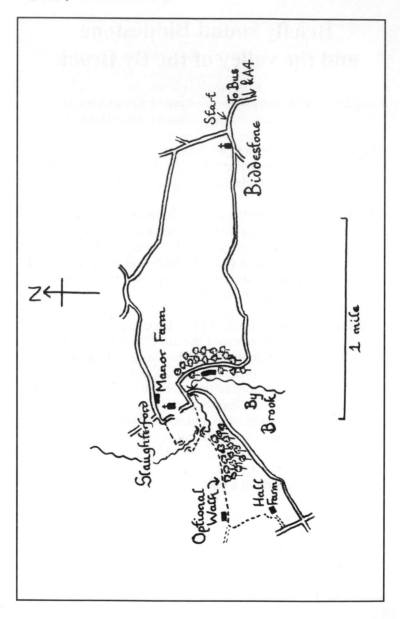

Itinerary

Biddestone has two pubs; The Biddestone Arms at the far east end of the village, about 100 yards from the trim 17th-century manor house with its brick gazebo and ornamental topiary, and The White Horse on the village green with another gazebo next door. This garden building is well appointed for people browsing as it has a fireplace. With such a village centre you can see why idle ladies would enjoy a little viewing house from which to see and perhaps be seen. Because almost every house around the pond is a picture postcard of 17th-century Cotswold vernacular with gables and mullioned windows, Willow House on the north side is a relief. It has cambered or segmental-headed sash windows and a pedimented doorcase – a bit of late provincial baroque with its 1730 date in the cartouche on the eaves pediment.

Walk along the main street and up Church Road past the coyly-sheltered village pump which looks like early 20th-century Arts and Crafts work, and continue to the church. St Nicholas sits low and has no tower, but its 13th-century bell-turret is much rarer. It was built to house the sanctus bell which would be rung three times at the points of consecration in the mass so that ploughmen and shepherds in the fields could cross themselves at the right time even though they could not attend the service. There are very few left now because England developed its unique, mathematical system of change ringing. This required six or eight bells and a tower to ring them in. It became so popular that many churches, particularly in this area, built big mediaeval-looking towers as late as the 1750s so that they could have their ringers. Nearby Sherston church tower is one of these – rebuilt in a Gothick-classical mixture in 1730 by a Gloucestershire mason-architect, Thomas Sumsion. Priston (Walk 7) has another Georgian tower of 1751. Inside our church, the nave is beautifully unrestored with Dickensian woodwork: high box pews, west gallery and planked waggon roof. There is a Norman font, a royal coat of arms in its appropriate place above the chancel arch and local benefaction boards that are worth reading. As you go out, look for a mass dial in the porch and work out what has gone wrong.

Fork right immediately outside the church gate along Challows Lane and follow the lane across a simplified landscape. This drops quite suddenly into a complex of wooded valleys with drifts of snowdrops in early spring. Down the hill turn right, go past the derelict paper mill complex on your left and, at the junction, don't cross the bridge but walk alongside the brook towards Slaughterford. This may have been where Alfred the Great slaughtered some Danes or it may be the ford of slates. If you take the optional extra walk you will see why the second derivation is likely.

At the first bend by a cottage row with a 1765 datestone, squeeze through the wooden pinch-bum stile where the notice says "Private Land, Public Footpath Only". This leads to a fascinating stretch. First comes an enormous mill wheel in a coppice with only sketchy remains of walls around it. Then you cross the old race and the By Brook itself, which runs quite formidably at this point. Both bridges and the following strip of land are very narrow.

Now there is a choice. For an extra two miles, and those slates, take the path up left along the fringe of the wood. This climbs steeply with expansive views and crosses the forecourt of a farmhouse whose sympathetic restoration would have satisfied William Morris. 20 years ago it was mere roofless walls, but it commands a wonderful valley view to the east and north so it was bought and the slow rescue begun. Fork left past Hall Farm onto a lane. Turn left here then shortly left again down a deeply-channelled lane back into the valley. The banks are composed of finely-divided limestone strata from which the slates must have tumbled almost ready-made. You will come out over the bridge back into Slaughterford again, though the paper-mill pool will tempt you to fish-spotting.

If you chose the shorter walk you would have continued along the river bank past a deep round pool of the river which is very tempting in summer. Above this is a modern sluice. Cross this, bolting the two gates after you, and head right by the electricity pole, uphill to the village. You regain the lane by keeping the two stone barns, the smaller of which is an

Bell Turret, Biddestone Church

unusual dovecote, on your right. The attractive, rambling Weaver's Cottage, also on your right, has an interesting long, blocked window which looks like an oriel.

In the field across the lane is St Nicholas's church. It was in ruins for 200 years after Cromwell's men ransacked it in the Civil War, but was rebuilt in 1823 and then restored in 1883. It is totally devoid of interest inside. As you walk left and up the hill, take the right-hand fork past Manor Farm and you will soon lose this enchantingly ragged area of country and be back to the flat lands and Biddestone again.

The Two Rivers Walk – Farleigh Hungerford Castle and the nearest England gets to the Loire Valley

Length: 5$^{1}/_{2}$ miles/Grade B (though there is so much to see that it should be Grade A)

Maps: O.S. Explorers 142 (Shepton Mallet & Mendip Hills East) & 143 (Warminster & Trowbridge)

Theme: Fisherman's country, deep waters, roaring weirs and high, wooded slopes with castles, manor houses and a delightful south-facing village. This really must be one of the most satisfying walks in England.

Transport: By car – take the A36 Warminster road out of Bath. Glimpse the Dundas Aqueduct as you pass, then turn left at the top of Limpley Stoke Hill for Freshford, and park thoughtfully, not in the narrower village streets (ST 791600).
By bus – there is an infrequent service to Freshford Post Office on No. 756 (excluding Wednesdays and Sundays).

Things to look out for:
1   Fish and fishermen: you'll see plenty of both
2   A knight sixteen feet high
3   Real lead coffins in a gloomy crypt
4   Britannia standing on a cutwater
5   A mediaeval study of Jesus crucified on a bush of flowers
6   An Italian hillside garden in Wiltshire
7   A dying Gaul on a wall
8   One of Britain's earliest factories

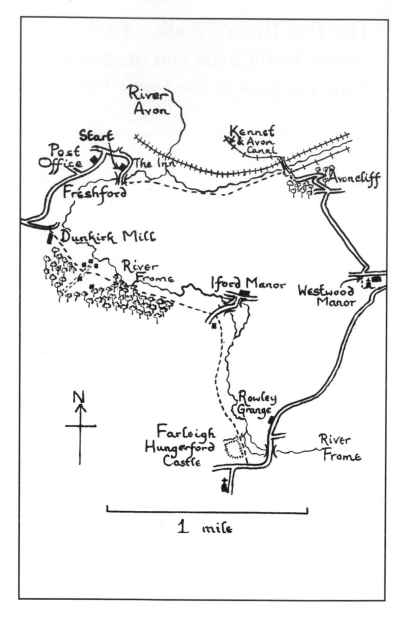

Itinerary

If you enjoy a variety of architecture you will not want to leave Freshford. Like so many places around Bath it is unusually rich. But cross the bridge over the Frome by The Inn because we will be coming back through the village.

Immediately over the bridge take the path left across the field. Soon you will be walking with the wider, heron-priested Avon on your left and woodland rising sharply on your right. Springtime here produces a riot of cherry blossom. Across the river are the railway and the Kennet & Avon Canal, but when you hear the weir roaring you will be in sight of John Rennie's splendid 1803 aqueduct which brings the canal in three stately strides over the river. The gaunt country house with the high wall was a workhouse and before that a 17th-century Flemish weavers' establishment with a domed drying shed to the rear. This is very early industrial planning.

If you are already thirsty and hungry Teazels Coffee Shop on this side, or The Cross Guns on the other side of the canal are both very welcoming, and next to the pub is the Canal Bookshop. To reach the pub go under the dry arch, otherwise your lane climbs steeply up right into the wood and takes you into Avoncliff. Cross the staggered cross-roads and continue towards Westwood. The church tower will be in sight all the time and a fine view across to the Westbury White Horse. When you reach the Old Malt House, the best route is by the path straight across the road. This gives you a good view of the back of the interesting but rather evasive Westwood Manor. Walls tend to shut it in but enjoy the Jacobean gateway with its strapwork cresting. It is managed by the National Trust and is open from 1 April to 30 September on Sundays, Tuesdays and Wednesdays from 2-5pm; £3.50 for adults and children.

St Mary's church is kept open and is full of good things. A stone devil with a gaping mouth hangs dramatically over the font. The east window has amazing 15th-century stained glass of Jesus crucified over a flower vase with dandelions and lilies behind him. The Perpendicular wooden roof of the side chapel is richly carved but the Georgian plaster vault to the nave would look more at home in a Bath drawing room. As you leave the churchyard look over the wall to see how the box avenue is now so overgrown that it almost blocks entry to the Manor.

Now comes a lonely stretch of road with the thin, high towers of Farleigh Hungerford Castle getting nearer and more picturesque at every turn. These two miles are really more like France than most of France. Don't miss Rowley Grange very close in on your right. It has a dovecote in its gable and great walled gardens. A right turn across the river and 300 traffic-ridden yards will bring you to the castle. It is open daily from 1 April to 31 October from 10-6pm, and from 1 November to 31 March from 10-4pm, except Mondays and Tuesdays; admission: adults £2.20, children £1.10.

The walls and towers look better from outside but St Leonard's chapel is the real reason for going in. It has a crypt out of Dracula with coffins in the dark and the chapel itself has a gigantic mural of St George in armour. There are other murals behind the whitewash waiting to be exposed, and in the Hungerford side chapel is a sumptuous 1648 white marble chest tomb of Sir Edward and Lady Margaret Hungerford. If you have time and are a church buff, it is worth a short extra walk along the main road, then left into the village to see the carefully restored church with four matching tombs like fancy Gothick cupboards set around the altar.

Between castle and river is a path close under the frowning walls leading past a trout farm; be careful on the little bridge. Then you have several fields to cross with the river, the Frome again, on your right. Tantalising glimpses of Iford's hill garden keep showing through the trees.

When you strike the lane your next path is over the stile opposite, but first you must go 100 yards to the right past the mill to stand on the bridge. Britannia has only been on the cutwater for 90 years though the bridge is over 600 years old. Iford Manor looks wonderful from this viewpoint: 1725 the main front, the outbuilding to the left rather older; behind them up the hill are the garden buildings and formal walks laid out

by the architect, Harold Peto, between 1899 and 1933. The Casita on the far right is genuine Italian work of about 1200 set up here in 1913; there are cloisters and lots of statuary and sculpture including a copy of the famous Dying Gaul. The layout is a perfect example of that fashion for fantastical architectural gardens which obsessed the Edwardians before the real nightmare of the First World War hit them. Iford is open from October to April on Sundays, and at Easter, from 2-5pm; from May to September daily, except Mondays and Fridays, 2-5pm; admission: adults £2.20, children £1.60.

Go back to the stile and enjoy a long peaceful stretch. Enter the wood at a gate and stile, cross two metal stiles, a tiny plank bridge by some cottages, and a final gate before reaching a sometimes muddy path to Dunkirk Mill, a fine early 18th-century block. The hill road up left is steep and you will be glad to take the first right onto a level road. Then follows half a mile through Freshford with literally dozens of dream retirement homes looking out over the valley view. The Old Parsonage of about 1650 is most romantic and there is an old pub, The Greyhound, now converted into a house – look out for its ironwork sign. Before you go home take in the early 18th-century house opposite the church with its broken pediment and charmingly amateur Ionic pilasters and look for a lion above a doorway round the corner. The house next to it, Corner House, has intersecting Gothick tracery in its windows but a classical fluted frieze. If you look carefully you will see that its long corner stones or quoins have been pitted to fix the colourwashed render which once brightened the façade, now it looks stripped and bare. One last house is worth considering – as you go downhill to the pub see how the Victorians have made a late 17th-century façade more Gothic with a fancy porch and dripstones with lions' heads over the cross-mullioned windows.

If you want to end your walk with a meal at The Inn it is almost always fully booked at the weekends so make sure you telephone (01225 722250) before you set out.

Combe Hay and Wellow –
the valleys of the two lost railways

Length: For motorists: 5¼ miles/Grade B
By bus: 6 miles/Grade B

Maps: O.S. Explorers 142 (Shepton Mallet & Mendip
Hills East) & 155 (Bristol & Bath)

Theme: This is deservedly the best-known walking country
around Bath, a blandly beautiful, almost Claudeian,
landscape where ruined viaducts and idyllic villages
are disposed about hanging woods and finely con-
toured hills; almost, perhaps, too English to be true.

Transport: By car – the A367 from Bath to Radstock dips
steeply down into the Cam valley at Dunkerton.
On the hill going up the other side take the narrow
left-hand lane signposted White Ox Mead. Park
thoughtfully near the first miniature crossroads
(ST 718584).
By bus – take Nos. 173, 175, 176 or 178 to Radstock
and ask for the first stop after Dunkerton. The
nearby signpost will direct you to White Ox Mead.

Things to look out for:
1   A piece of modern Chinoiserie over a stream
2   A lock of the Somersetshire Coal Canal
3   A village on which arguably too much money has been spent
4   Solid evidence of a high standard of literacy in 15th-century
England
5   A whole plague of pitching eyes
6   One of the first and most brutalist Perpendicular church towers
7   St Philip with three loaves of bread

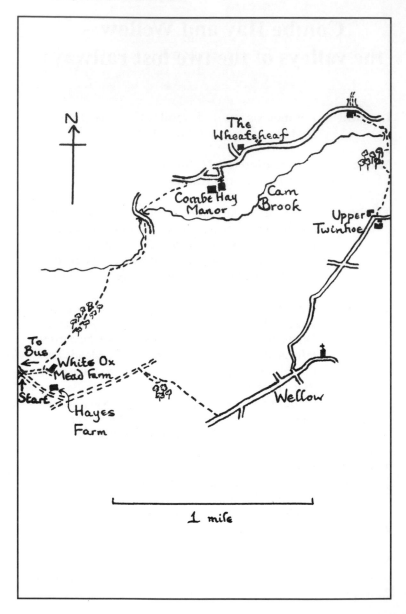

N

The Wheatsheaf

Combe Hay Manor

Cam Brook

Upper Twinhoe

To Bus

White Ox Mead Farm

Start

Hayes Farm

Wellow

1 mile

Itinerary

When you reach the miniature cross-roads take the left-hand downhill lane and turn left off it onto the public footpath before you reach the farm. There is a deep combe leading down into the valley, but take the occasionally muddy right-hand track that descends more gently through a copse and open fields to the Cam Brook. The last stage of the path runs along the bank of the stream and is somewhat waterworn. A lane will bridge you across the Brook, then take the gate immediately on your right. High above you on the left is the pink-washed *cottage orné* lodge to Combe Hay Manor which is in the trees at the end of the drive to your right. Make towards the drive, climbing the hill diagonally and a stile will lead you into the village, an affluent but rewarding place.

Turn right and walk towards the church. Stradling Barn has huge pitching eyes for the hay and has been well converted apart from the usual dark-stained hardwood frames to the openings. More eyes in barns and stables overlook the little church. If you stand by the hedge at the east end you can admire the elegant, spare neo-Classical east front of the Manor with its sash windows cut sharply without surrounds into the smooth golden ashlar. Its architect is unknown, but the 1780s design is certainly self-denying enough to be by George Steuart or perhaps the great James Wyatt himself. Now go to the west tower and look at the return, or side, façade of the house and you will see the heavy bolection cornice and Bath-style moulded surrounds to the windows which are much earlier in date and reveal the original building phase of the 1730s. John Strahan, the Bristol architect much abused by John Wood who called him "piratical", has been suggested as the architect of this section. Walkers should bear in mind that the house is strictly private property and they should not trespass inside its grounds. Down in the valley below there is a modern commemorative obelisk and a red Chinese bridge spanning the brook.

The church is usually locked so enjoy the chest tombs and look for the stone coffin with a fabric top complete with

31

dangling tassels. Then on your way out of the village down the valley it is worth comparing the Old Rectory with Rectory House. The original rector's house is sedate and uninspiring whereas its modern replacement appears to have grown organically out of its rock garden and has a dramatic projecting terrace – a minor example of Frank Lloyd Wright in Somerset. In fact the modern houses in this valley are all most encouraging. At this mid point in the walk The Wheatsheaf pub is worth a stop if you are thirsty. It has charming nesting boxes for pigeons and doves alongside its upper windows. Go past the pub and as you take the right-hand fork you will see a blue brick railway bridge on the left-hand road. Underneath is the old Cam Valley branch of the Great Western Railway which will keep you company for the next beautifully wooded stretch.

The next large arch on the left under the railway embankment was built to allow the Somersetshire Coal Canal through which brought coal from the North Somerset coalfields to Bath and beyond. A bill was passed for its construction in 1794; there is an Industrial Buildings Trust notice under the arch which will tell you more about the canal. Bridge Farm across the road was probably a lock keeper's house. Cross the road, take the stile and you will find yourself on a broad green shelf where the canal once ran. This ends in the brambly, but well preserved, stone walls of a lock. One path goes on down the valley to more canal remains, but we cross the stream and climb the steep track up into Twinhoe.

Straight on here, over a cross-roads and down again will bring you into Wellow with exciting views of the viaduct of the second 'lost' line, once the Somerset and Dorset main route to Bath from Bournemouth, Evercreech and Radstock. This had the notorious Combe Down tunnel which used to suffocate the occasional driver!

Turn left at the junction and make for the church. St Julian's was paid for by the first Speaker of the House of Commons and the hard uncompromising lines of its tower suggest that the early designers in Perpendicular Gothic were

Viaduct near Wellow

as keen on harsh geometry in 1372 as any of our modern architects. And here the Victorians – Bodley and Garner – were unusually tactful in their chancel addition of 1890 which continues the brutal lines of the main building. The key for the church is kept at Footman's Cottage opposite the Fox and Badger pub on the main street. Inside, the woodwork is rich and the implication of the ledges on every bench is interesting. Some social historians try to deduce from these that most of the rural population was literate as far back as the 15th century, and carried missals to church with them to follow the service. It seems just as likely that they had gloves and mufflers or even took a snack with them to munch if the service was over long. Nobody can be sure. Most of the rood screen is original but the loft is a later addition. Its survival in any shape, together with the strapwork-decorated font cover of Archbishop Laud's time, is an indication that this was a High Church parish in the Low Church, early 17th-century period. Before you leave the church take a look in the Hungerford Chapel to view the sinister effigy of Dorothy Popham and then look up and see if you can spot Christ and his twelve Apostles on the wall. The subject is unique in English mediaeval wall painting.

It may seem carping, but most of the old cottages in Wellow have been restored so thoroughly that the village lacks texture. Combe Hay has more modern building yet sits more easily in its landscape. Wellow has declared war on lichen, roughcast and old lime mortar. What is cheering, however, is that the village children can still use the 1852 school, now St Julian's primary. Before you set off back to White Ox Mead don't forget the Fox and Badger which is handy for refreshment.

Walk through the village until the houses end and take the second right-hand track before the electric power lines. This is signposted, but then you have to follow the hedge uphill. Pass through a small metal gate and turn left to a wooden stile. The right of way goes diagonally right, across the next large field, but if it is sown, cross under the power lines to the right-hand edge of the wood and follow the hedge round until you

St Julian's Church, Wellow

reach a track. Left here, then fork right, back into White Ox Mead. The first house you come to, Hayes Farm, is nothing remarkable architecturally, but with its comfortable orchard garden and homely, worn roughcast on rubble stone walls, it is so much at home in its rural setting that the villagers of Wellow could profitably walk here to study it. Affluence does not always produce sensitive aesthetics.

The valley of the Mells River and Barrow Hill

Length: 5¹/₂ miles/Grade B

Map: O.S. Explorer 142 (Shepton Mallet & Mendip Hills East)

Theme: An area of countryside haunted by its past, often uncomfortably so. The oversensitive should walk warily here: a beautiful village where the aristocratic paternalism of the 19th century has lingered, and a strange rocky valley where opposing industrial forces of the same period have left their sinister traces. There is an excellent pub at Mells in which to recover, but book in advance if you want to eat.

Transport: By car – take the A367 to Radstock and then the A362 Frome road. Turn right 4 miles out of Radstock for Vobster, then follow the signs to Mells. As you enter the village, turn right opposite the little bus shelter. Go 250 yards down this lane and park in the spacious layby on the right (ST 726490). By bus – The No.184 Frome bus runs every two hours (except on Sundays) and stops in Mells.

Things to look out for:
1 Country where working railways pop in and out of tunnels like toys on a giant scale
2 A bronze man riding a bronze horse in a church
3 15th-century town planning
4 The relics of a miniature Sheffield
5 A plaster peacock by Burne Jones
6 A lot of minor Lutyens architecture in one small place
7 A prehistoric mystery of rivalry

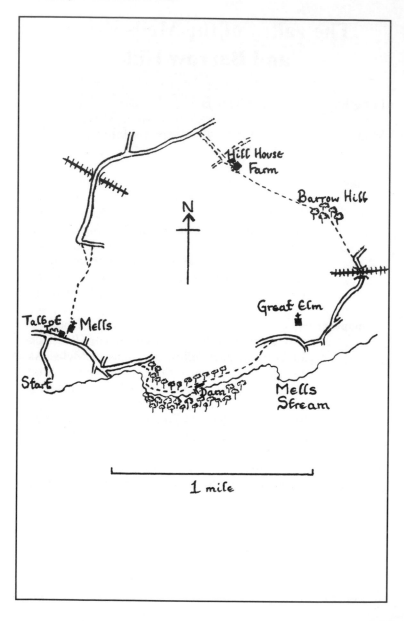

Itinerary

The lane where you begin will get you into the odd atmosphere of Mells. There is a village lock-up still intact with its iron peep-grille and a dry grotto in a wall, but it is the general condition of village houses like Poyntz House and Poyntz Cottage which is most remarkable. Hardly any of the houses in Mells have been done up or commuterised. The walls, the windows and the thatch are all as they were 100 years ago and that is a real rarity. Look out for the 1598 datestone on No. 1 Garston Gate and the traces of ox blood colour wash on the house next door. The Pre-Raphaelite painter, Sir Edward Burne Jones, often stayed in Mells with his friend and favourite model, Lady Frances Horner. He loved the colour of these cottages and praised them for "their holy greyness".

Back at the bus shelter turn right with glimpses of the 16th-century Manor House and the filigree elegance of St Andrew's tower over walls to your left and an early 18th-century façade to your right. As you turn left by the pleasant Talbot Inn, the street to the church gate is what is left of a town planning scheme of 1470 by John Selwood, Abbot of Glastonbury. Nos. 4 and 6 are the least altered, but you will get a much richer feeling of the mediaeval past in the sheltered inner courtyard of the inn which backs onto these 15th-century houses. Don't miss a jowly portrait of Queen Victoria and a chained dog – a talbot taken from the Horners' coat of arms.

The Horner family, descendants of Little Jack Horner, lived in the Manor House and in the Edwardian period gathered a select collection of friends and artists around them called the Souls. Even if you have a cheerful nature you should spend some time in the church and graveyard. The south porch is one of the most beautiful in the county with an almost Chinese sweep to its roofline and emaciated crocketed pinnacles. Inside the church on your left is a Pre-Raphaelite-style embroidery by Lady Horner and, under the tower, an 1886 Burne Jones plaster monument with a peacock commemorating Laura Lyttelton. In the Horner chapel the horrors of the First World War are tangible. There is a bronze of horse and rider high on a stone plinth in memory of Edward Horner who was killed at Noyelles in 1917 at the age of 28 – a strange but intensely moving thing to see inside a church. Also, on the wall, the grave marker of Raymond Asquith who died of wounds in 1916.

Outside to the east of the church are the graves designed by Lutyens and Eric Gill of Siegfried Sassoon, the War poet; Ronald Knox, the translator; a Liberal cabinet minister; and, inevitably, the Horners. Walk around to the yew avenue, another Lutyens creation, and spare a glance for the rare, early Arts and Crafts wooden stile with moving parts in the graveyard wall, one of only three surviving in the country, patented by Thomas Lyne of Malmesbury in 1857.

Back at the the Talbot turn left and walk down to the War Memorial. Lutyens consciously avoided denominational symbols in his memorials so that heroes of any religion could be honoured; he gave this one a column with St George killing the dragon. Walk downhill to the stone slate shelter set diagonally to the road, Lutyens again, and then take the road on the left sign-posted Great Elm. After 250 yards turn right along the track beside the Mells River. This will drop you into an entirely different world, not of the Horners, the gentlemen landowners, but the Fussells, the ironmasters who turned this area upside down with their industrial enterprises between 1820 and 1870.

The rocks close in, gloomy and unexpectedly high, and the stream flows deep and dark beside the track. Above you on the left the cliffs are topped by Wadbury Camp, first of a mysterious cluster of ancient fortifications. If you look closely you can make out a narrow road "made at immense labour for the cavalry to go down the rocks to the river". But then the first industrial ruins come into sight by a damned stretch of the river. Travellers have sometimes camped here among the snowdrops and wild garlic making it even more atmospheric. The path threads past old water channels and crumbling walls, all shadowed by dense trees. Across the river is Tedbury, another ancient camp. Legend tells of a battle near here where two kings perished, so these may have been their rival strongholds.

Great Elm Church

Then the Fussell land ends with the villas of Great Elm. Keep down by the river until the footpath rises to a lane.

If you enjoy railways it is worth a brief detour here down the hill, over the stream and right into the woods to see the quarry lines in their romantic setting. Otherwise turn right into the village and at least peer through the low windows of the church which, with its Jacobean box pews and west gallery, is one of those that time (and the Victorians) has forgotten. Back on the main street turn left towards Buckland Dinham by the pretty 1835 Providence Chapel with its Gothick-arched windows and chequerboard of leaded panes. It is now The Old Chapel and has been tactfully converted into a house. Follow the lane until yet another quarry line passes over it, then take the first track on the left, going uphill. Over the stile, follow the hedge until you see a dark coppice on the hill above you. The next stile, an awkward one, is just to the left of this. It brings you out on Barrow Hill with wide views of this attractively ravaged landscape including the lonely chimney of Buckland Dinham colliery. Cross the stile in the next fence and make for the big white farmhouse three fields away. The first field is a big one, but in its far right-hand corner you will find a rough track between hedges again, which can be muddy. The designated footpath follows this track to Hill House farm, passing along the left-hand walls onto the farm driveway.

The drive shortly crosses over a rough bridleway and leads out onto a lane. Turn left and enjoy the far-reaching views from Gare Hill in the south-east, past Alfred's Tower at Stourhead to Creech Hill in the south-west. Follow the lane over a railway bridge and at a sharp left-hand bend, cross the stone stile. The right of way crosses the field diagonally, but if this has been sown, you may prefer to walk a further 200 yards along the lane before taking another path along the left-hand side of the field. Go through the gap at the far corner, cross straight on to the gate in the next hedge and make straight for Mells church, entering the graveyard through the Arts and Crafts stile.

Camerton Village and the greened-over coal mines of the Cam Brook

Length: For motorists: 5¹/₂ miles/Grade B
By bus (see below): 7 miles/Grade A

Maps: O.S. Explorer 142 (Shepton Mallet &Mendip Hills East) and 155 (Bristol & Bath)

Theme: To explore the overgrown railway lines, lost canal, wooded spoil tips and fascinating industrial relics of what was a smoky, bustling coalfield producing 140,000 tons a year only a short time ago. This is a walk of historical rather than picturesque interest.

Transport: By car – take the A367 Radstock road and fork right onto the B3115 for Timsbury. After another three miles take the Camerton turn left. Down the valley and up the other side, then follow signs to the church on your left. Park in the car-park on the right of Church Lane (ST 685574).
By bus – take Nos. 173, 175, 176 or 178 for Radstock as far as the Camerton turn. Your road goes right and you have ³/₄ of a mile to walk. No. 772 operates direct to Camerton on Tuesdays and Wednesdays but you will have to return by the Radstock route.

Things to look out for:
1 An elephant and a rhinoceros on a church tower
2 The Somersetshire Coal Canal dug in 1800 that turned into a railway in 1910
3 Old mines turned into forests
4 What happened when a church choir got tipsy for five days
5 The remains of a G.S.Repton arboretum
6 A 1951 Festival of Britain mining relic

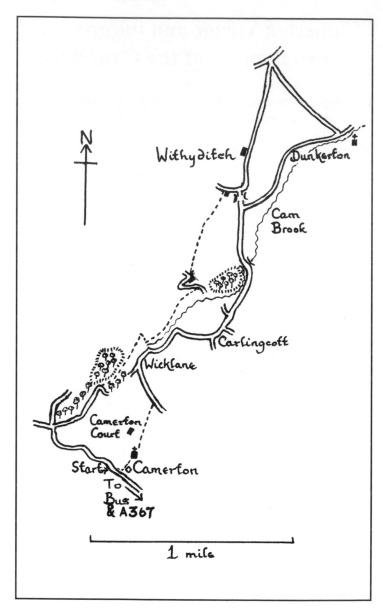

N

Withyditch

Dunkerton

Cam
Brook

Carlingcott

Wicklane

Camerton
Court

Start → ↔ Camerton
To
Bus →
& A367

1 mile

Itinerary

The Old Rectory you have just passed was where the *Journal of a Somerset Rector* was written by the Revd. John Skinner. He wrote about this area in the 1820s when 9,000 miners worked in the coalfield. Walk down the lane to the church and on your left are views of the formal gardens laid out in what was the stable yard of Camerton Court; you will see box hedges, a circular temple, pyramidal-roofed garden houses and lead statues – see if you can spot Mercury. St Peter's is usually locked so if you want to go inside ask for the key at the aggressively-styled new rectory by the car-park. The church has a rigorously brutalist Perpendicular tower with extraordinary carved stops to the hoodmoulds over its windows. There is a man with a lute serenading a woman, several monstrous beasts and, on the north side, an elephant and rhinoceros. Inside is a statue of a girl lying down. This was originally outside the porch so that the young man who broke her heart could see it every time he went to church. The Carew Chapel is dated 1638 on the outside wall. It has a tomb chest to Sir John and his wife of 1640 which is Jacobean, but the other of 1683, with the sulky mourning figure at the side, is Classical.

Skinner tells how a new vein of coal was found on a Wednesday and that set off such a drinking bout that his Camerton church choir were still drunk on Sunday morning so he turned them out of church. They were so angry that they joined the Methodists who built a new gallery to accommodate them.

Take the iron gate out at the bottom of the churchyard and you are in a great natural ampitheatre scattered with the specimen trees – wellingtonias and cedars – that George Stanley Repton, son of the famous landscape gardener, Humphry, planted in 1838 to surround Camerton Court. The house has a fine Ionic loggia and greenhouse and the present owner is busy adding gravel paths and cascades to the landscape. The path goes straight down the valley to the lane. Turn left there and you will see the old spoil heaps perking up ahead covered in woodland – mostly pines. Go right at the next T-junction along

Wick Lane. Here are miners' cottages with their backs to you and all their windows facing north to the colliery.

The lane climbs steeply up through Carlingcott with little streams running down between a mix of old cottages with ovolo mullions – look for these at the Physiotherapy clinic – and later miners' houses with Welsh slate roofs and plastic-framed windows. The Beehive was an unpretentious miners' pub when this book first appeared, but now it is a private house. Look out for the 1851 Methodist Chapel which is keeping the mining tradition of non-conformity alive.

Go straight on past the chapel at the top of the hill then take the right-hand fork past Victoria Cottages, with their strange heritage plaque, all the way down again across a bridge with an iron sign forbidding heavy 'Locomotives' to cross. Turn right along the lower road into Dunkerton. Here there is a dull church, but the house overlooking it across the valley was charmingly Gothicized with bow windows in the Regency. As you turn sharp left uphill before this house, you will see the embankments either side where the canal and railway once bridged the lane. The name Viaduct Cottage will help you spot these industrial relics. They must have overshadowed Crooked Cottage on the left, an attractive building of 1695 with ovolo mullions and oval windows.

As soon as you reach the main road at the top of the hill take the lane on the left back down again. You pass the School House on the right with a child kneeling in prayer on its gable end and then Withyditch Baptist Chapel where there is still "A Warm Welcome to All". The Old Farmhouse has ovolo mullions, a steep pantile roof and a sumptuous shell hood over the door. Around 1690 this valley must already have been prosperous.

A little further along the lane you can see the old canal-rail bed in the field below with a half-buried brick bridge over a shallow depression. But turn right, up the hill, before this submerged bridge and take the path on the left through the iron gate past the first cottage. From now on you will be looking down on the old canal bed above a wooded spoil heap. The

Cottage range at entrance to Camerton Court

path goes through another iron gate, straight across a grassy field to a three-barred wooden stile and diagonally across the next large field. Go down round the steep bend with old miners' houses, cross the canal-rail bed, but before you cross the Cam Brook take the second field path on the right. This runs between brook and rail bed to a second lane. Bear right up this between the three cottages and look around you. This was the basin of the old canal and for a time it was the railhead of the G.W.R. line that served the top of the valley from Hallatrow to Camerton and opened in 1882. In 1895 the canal that ran alongside it was doing so badly that the company offered to sell the stretch you have just been following. The Somerset and Dorset Railway declined and eventually the G.W.R. bought the canal and in 1910 opened the railway right down to Limpley Stoke. However, passenger traffic only lasted until 1917.

The path runs between the two left-hand houses. The high bank you follow across the field is all that is left of rail and canal. The two wooded spoil heaps on your right were Camerton 1 and Camerton 2 collieries. As you pass the first there is a good stretch of railway on the left with two bridges over the brook. The path joins the road and on the right is the best row of miners' cottages in the valley, of grey rubble masonry. Above these were the old railway sidings.

You reach the main road after half a mile. Turn right and just a little way up is a stile on the right leading into Camerton's 'Heritage Site', built on the course of the Somersetshire Coal Canal. A map explains all the industrial remains you have seen. There is also a huge statue of a miner, cast from one that featured in the 1951 Festival of Britain and originally set up in front of The Jolly Collier pub. The pub has now been converted into a private house and surrounded by the new housing of Collier Close. The miner, once coal black, was removed to his new site in 1991 and is now, inexplicably, painted rust red.

As both pubs on this walk have been closed since the first edition of this book your only chance for refreshment is at The Camerton Inn on the B3115.

Priston Mill and the Conygre Valley

Length: For motorists: 5¹/₂ miles/Grade B
By bus (see below): 6¹/₂ miles/Grade A

Map: O.S. Explorer 155 (Bristol & Bath)

Theme: A plunge into rough deep country on the very outskirts of Bath, with unspoilt valleys, two good villages and Priston Mill, an extraordinary working survival which is like a cross between a rustic idyll and something from a horror movie. The Mill is only open after Easter at bank holiday wekends, and on Thursdays in August.

Transport: By car – Englishcombe is just beyond the Bath suburbs. Take the A367 Radstock road. Turn right by the Red Lion inn at the Odd Down roundabout. After a mile, take Padleigh Hill, the narrow left turn for Englishcombe, and park in the village near the church (ST 716628).
By bus – No. 772 operates to Englishcombe on Wednesdays and Thursdays only; otherwise take the Nos. 10 or 11 to Southdown School, then follow the Englishcombe sign down the steep hill.

Things to look out for:
1 Duchy of Cornwall signs – much of this area belongs to Prince Charles
2 A hamlet that says "Take me or leave me"
3 Perhaps the most excitingly sinister mill wheel still working in England
4 A boundary between two kingdoms
5 The fattest weathercock in the area
6 A bible-thumping inscription
7 How to tell one mullion from another

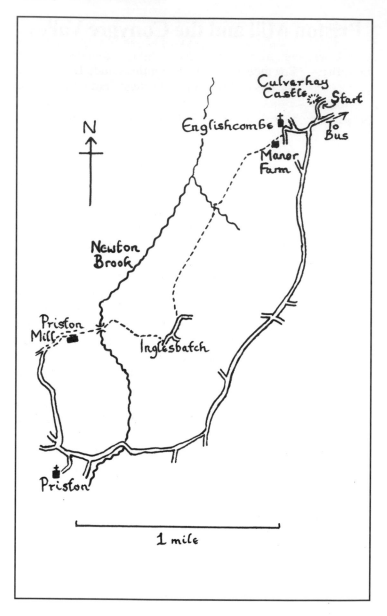

N↑

Culverhay Castle   Start

Englishcombe

To Bus

Manor Farm

Newton Brook

Priston Mill

Inglesbatch

Priston

1 mile

Itinerary

If you are travelling by bus and you enjoy prehistoric earthworks then turn right down Washpool Lane and walk up to Nursery View, the raw red houses on a little hill, to look down into Culverhay Castle. This fortification was built on the line of Woden's Dyke, or the Wansdyke, which gives its name to this area of North Somerset. Englishcombe church also stands on the dyke which you can trace running north-west downhill from the churchyard; it was dug in the Dark Ages.

St Peter's is a Norman three-cell of nave, tower and chancel. It still has a corbel table of weird carvings around the east end. These Norman corbel tables are always interesting because the figures are violent, grotesque or rude. Rude ones are called *Sheila na Gigs* but Puritans tended to smash these. Here you will find a horse that might be a Saxon idol and a man pulling a silly face. The church was probably rebuilt in the 18th century as the tower has fine squared masonry, angular crocketted pinnacles and distinctly un-mediaeval mouldings; the chancel was no doubt refaced at the same time. St Peter's is kept locked but there is a notice in one of the windows listing the key-holders. From the churchyard you have a fine view over the valley towards Culverhay Castle.

Before you turn right on the lane above the church, look carefully at the house and barn on your left. The barn has a roof of terracotta pantiles like a waving sea and there are more, double Roman, clay tiles on the outshut to the road. The gable end has a circular window with three elegantly carved arms of tracery and there are stepped slates projecting from the wall to throw water onto the outshut roof. The Tithe Barn is open on bank holidays and Sundays from Easter to September (3-5.30pm). The squared masonry of the barn is far superior to that of the house alongside which is much younger and built of rubble stone with a thin coating of render. There are ovolo-moulded mullions which are 17th-century and small but elegant 18th-century gate-piers.

Walk along the lane towards Manor Farm which, with its contemporary complex of ruggedly attractive farm buildings, was built in 1869 and soon you are in deep, old Somerset. The track turns to a path, sometimes muddy, which dives down a deep valley to a wooden causeway over the stream and up again on the other side. At the right time of year this lovely lost country is a great place for flowers. Green-winged orchids are very choosey about which year to flower in, but if you are not lucky with these increasingly rare plants there are primroses and bluebells in generous quantities. One other flower used to grow in great numbers in this area but unfortunately its young shoots were delicious when boiled; known locally as Bath asparagus, bunches of it were sold at market. It was eventually eaten into great rarity, so it never does to take any wild flower for granted in this heavily populated country.

Then you come to a scatter of farms and houses called Inglesbatch. There is manure everywhere and tall metal silos soar above the barns. Most of the cottages and even the old chapel have been done up for commuters. Whether you like it is a matter of taste, but in its way it is unspoilt and real. You hit a surfaced road again here but do not take either left turns. Go straight on down into Mill Lane. This soon turns into a track and ends in a big downhill field. Below in the valley you can see Priston Mill, the real high spot of this walk. Follow the telegraph poles to a stile lurking in the bottom hedge, then make for the iron footbridge to your left over the river and you will reach the Mill through its farmyard with the neat late 18th-century mill house above you. The field you have just crossed was a water meadow and the dry channel across the mill house garden once led to a system of sluices that kept several fields green in dry weather.

The Mill has a shop for its produce, The Granary, in the barn to the rear and it serves light refreshments. It is open on Easter Sunday and Monday, bank holiday Sundays and Mondays, and Thursday afternoons in August (admission: adults £2.50, children £1.75). It is the hidden wheel that will stay in your memory. Unlike most mill wheels it is inside the building, though you can glimpse it in its dark recess if you go down the steps. Technically it is an overshot pitch-back wheel, made of iron, 27 feet 10 inches in diameter and about 130 years old, though the Mill itself was here in 931AD. Prince Charles

Weathercock on St Luke's Church, Priston

owns it and it still grinds corn. If you are lucky you will see it start up while you are inside. A rush of smelly water pours out of an iron pipe and slowly the blades begin to turn. You can imagine the villain plunging to his death down in the churning water. It has the authentic smell and feel of Chaucer's England.

Walk along the mill race then turn left up the hill and into Priston. There is a pub, The Ring O' Bells (closed at lunchtime on Mondays, Wednesdays and Thursdays) and the village is a good place for spotting the difference between the late 17th-century ovolo-moulded mullions and the later, 18th-century edge-moulded mullions. See too if you can spot a lost pub – look out for a metal holder which has lost its sign. St Luke's church is securely padlocked but most of the interest is outside. The tower is a fascinating fake, a 1751 attempt at the Norman style of the original church. Its three boldly receding stages, plain Y-tracery in round-headed openings and balustrade around the top give the 18th-century date away. It may be only 250 years old, but the fabulously fat-bottomed weathercock makes up for that. Before you leave the churchyard take a look at Thomas Watts's stern warning of 1589 on the porch gable – "Priston Repent and Believe the Gospel" – and another Norman corbel table around the west end.

Just across the lane from the church is an 18th-century brick granary built on staddle stones, the 'mushrooms' you often see now used as garden ornaments, but intended originally to present an insoluble acrobatic problem for greedy rats and mice. Make your way out of the village passing Village Farm on your left which has a curious little Gothick building next to it. Was it a wayside chapel, or a garden house or a Regency cottage? The road rises steeply uphill and then you are on the lonely heights with wide views down left into the rough country you have been travelling. Half-way back to Englishcombe look out for Westvale on your left which has a modern sculpture of a flying angel playing a lute just like one of the symbols on the Tower of the Winds in Athens. After another mile or so you either turn left to the church and your car or go straight on past the Salem chapel and the forlorn Victorian school to the crossroads and the bus.

The Wansdyke Walk – Newton St Loe, Corston and Stanton Prior

Length: 6^1/$_2$ miles/Grade A

Map: O.S. Explorer 155 (Bristol & Bath)

Theme: This is King Arthur country of windy downlands and sudden camp-crowned hills where you can still recreate, through their long-drawn lines of battle, the stubborn Dark Age conflicts of Saxons and Britons.

Transport: By car – take the A4 Bristol road to the roundabout at The Globe inn, turn back sharply to the left and then, half-way up the hill, right into Newton St Loe village. Park by the church (ST 702649). By bus – The Nos. X39, 336, 337 or 339 will drop you at The Globe inn and you can start your walk there, visiting Newton St Loe on the way back.

Things to look out for:
1 The same grim Mendip handsomeness in a farmhouse of 1700 and one of 1980
2 A fondness for fossil ammonites
3 A barton
4 The Wansdyke itself (and sometimes you need to look hard for it!)
5 A lodge that deliberately echoes its gateposts
6 The canted bay of the English Rococo
7 A ha-ha

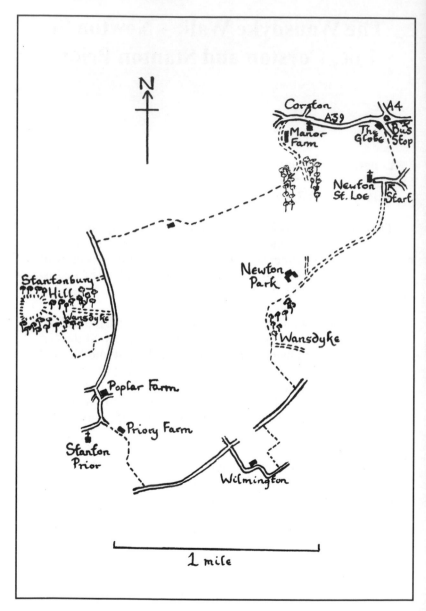

Itinerary

Newton St Loe, where you start out if you come by car, has a surprising hint of a little Tuscan hill town with its square of fine buildings just below the church. There is the former Free School, built and endowed by Richard Jones in 1698, a William and Mary building which proves that country people were not indifferent then to education. Its dripstones over the windows have been run together to form a string course and the robust arched hood on carved brackets over the door is another move towards classical forms. Stonewalls, the slightly later house opposite, makes a similar gesture towards the new style with its shallow eaves pediment. See if you can spot its date, 1715, on the sundial. Holy Trinity is worth a look for its 14th-century ball-flower ornament on the nave capitals and a pompous baroque monument to the Langtons of Newton Park. The cast-iron railings marking the vault are probably the earliest in Somerset. And don't miss the beautifully embroidered altar frontal with its symbols of Christ's passion sewn in gold thread.

Perhaps the best part of the square is its lower side with The Old Rectory, set in its own grounds with cedars and yews. It is now the Duchy of Cornwall office and you'll see the Duchy's crest on many of the farms on this walk. The Rectory was an 18th-century building given a mellow, round-arched façade in that brief Williamane period (1830-37) which preceded the Victorian free-for-all. Turn right and walk down a short step to the village square to enjoy a thatched cottage, rare for this area, and the green which commemorates the coronation of Elizabeth II.

Retrace your steps and turn down by the way you came in and take the short cut across the field to The Globe inn. Then turn left along the main Wells road to Corston. Just past the Corston village sign you will see an 1827 cast-iron Turnpike Trust marker set at the parish boundary. Pass the dull church and opposite Ashton Hill turn left down a little lane. You are suddenly in a different world. In an area of fine farmhouses Manor Farm is outstanding – a commanding nine-bay presence with cross-mullioned windows below, sashes above, a fine shell hood and a mounting block by the courtyard wall. The landscapes up this lane are a world apart from the busy main road.

You climb up past a wood and find yourself looking down into the deep valleys of the Newton Park estate with the garden front of the great house visible to the left. It was designed for Joseph Langton in 1761 by the oddly named architect, Stiff Leadbetter. The severe canted bay is typical of the mid-18th-century English Rococo style which kept its ornate decoration for the interior and allowed spectacular views out to the landscape.

This is an area of excellent two-step stiles; these mark your way past the lonely barton and along the left-hand field hedge to the lane. Stantonbury Hill looms close now, tree-covered, an Iron Age fort which, with Winsbury Hill beyond, was used as a strong-point when the Britons rallied against the invading Saxons around 470 AD. Ambrosium had the Wansdyke dug – a 50-mile rampart to protect the south-west – and finally Arthur defeated the Saxons at Mount Badon near Bath.

Turn left along the lane and, when you come to the second farm track on the right climbing up Stantonbury, stop and look around. This track follows the Wansdyke with the defensive ditch on its right. As it reaches the trees the track crosses over and uses the ditch. If you look the other way you can see Park Farm high on the hill. That marks the south-eastern course of the dyke which we will cross later.

If you wish to climb Stantonbury Hill, the way up is a new path a little further on. Cross the stile on the right, and follow the left-hand side of the hedge. When you reach the far corner of the field on your right, cross through the gap and follow the right-hand side of the hedge leading straight up to the wood. Back along the wood a short distance and you will find the way up through the trees and onto the fort. Otherwise, continue along the lane to Stanton Prior.

At the next cross-roads is Poplar Farm, an 18th-century house with a Regency façade of slick ashlar where you can buy honey. Look out for the ammonite near the entrance to Priory Farm and then walk up to the church. St Lawrence had an 1869 restoration so all the plaster is gone from the walls,

The Free School at Newton St Loe

but the Victorians decorated it with stencilling and numinous inscriptions. Fortunately they left the 15th-century waggon roof in the nave and a fascinating, if gruesome, Commonwealth monument of a husband and wife sitting either side of a table with a skull.

Now take the track past Priory Farm and climb the very steep, and sometimes watery, path over the down with great views to reach a lane. Left along this for half a mile, then right into Wilmington with a completely different valley-scape and views across to Inglesbatch (Walk 7). The old farmhouse here has been replaced with a modern house that recalls in its assertive character, Manor Farm, Corston. Cut back left by the field path alongside the last houses of the hamlet. The path clings to the right-hand hedges of the big field and brings you back to the earlier lane. Follow this to the right until you reach a two-step stile on the left.

Simply to return via the grounds of Bath Spa University College at Newton Park is easy. You follow the hedge down to the wood and playing field, and then bear right, through the new buildings and across the front of the house. To see the best stretch of the Wansdyke is, however, slightly harder. The dyke is in the field on your right as you go down the hill. Here the defensive ditch really looks deep enough for a Saxon to notice it. But it is better then to follow the dyke by the farm track down to the wood and playing fields as the path south-east of the house across the ha-ha has vanished. In amongst the modern lecture rooms is the old keep of a castle reclad in the 16th century. Then come the wide open Palladian-style arms of the main house and the right-hand fork of the drive leading back to Newton St Loe village. Even if you are tired, the lightly stylized gables of the Gothic lodge are a final architectural pleasure to end the walk and The Globe inn is handy for refreshment.

Hill paths and tow paths – Lansdown, North Stoke and Kelston

Length: 6^1/$_2$ miles/Grade A

Map: O.S. Explorer 155 (Bristol & Bath)

Theme: An Iron Age walk through Kelston and North Stoke, respectively the stoniest and loneliest villages in this area. A lovely walk too, though almost on the doorstep of Bath, with great views, great contrasts and some steady uphill climbing.

Transport: By car – head for Bristol, not on the main A4 but on the parallel A431 on the north side of the Avon. At Kelston (3^1/$_2$ miles), turn left at the house with a tower and park in the wide cul-de-sac leading down to the church (ST 699670).
     By bus – Nos. 319, 332 or 632 will drop you in Kelston village and you can see the church down the lane towards the river.

Things to look out for:

1   Dinghy racing on the Avon
2   A *Watership Down*-full of rabbits
3   A village with probably 2,500 years of continuous habitation
4   The realities of an Iron Age 'camp'
5   Clay pigeon shooting
6   A railway you are encouraged to walk on
7   A 18th-century brass foundry

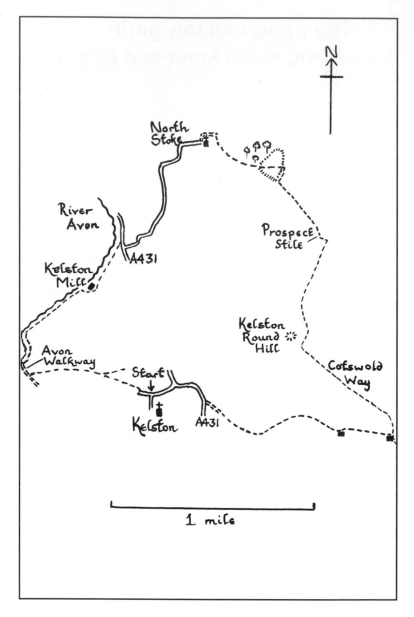

1 mile

Itinerary

St Nicholas church at Kelston is kept locked and has little of interest inside. The porch is a mini archaeological museum of fragments of Gothic tracery and a Roman coffin found at Park Farm. Walk around the churchyard for all the interest. First there is the splendid barn, bigger and finer than the church, with its beautiful stone slate roof and prominent midstrey or transept. Then at the east end is the vista of pale grey walls in this stoniest of villages. Kelston Tower House, the attractive Italianate villa like an inland lighthouse, was built in 1835 by the hugely wealthy Joseph Neeld of Grittleton in Wiltshire. He used it as a love nest for his French mistress and their love child, Anne Maria. In the field below you are the green terraces where the Great House of the Harringtons once stood and where Queen Elizabeth dined with Sir John Harrington in 1592 under the fountains playing in the courtyard. Sir John had real talent as a hydraulics engineer and invented the flushing water closet. From the extension to the churchyard you can see, across the fields, John Wood the Younger's Kelston Park, built in the 1770s. The old walled garden of the manor survives, now choked with elder and reeking of the rank smell of foxes. In the farmyard is the large, gabled dovecote that once supplied the manor with pigeon pies. The banding of its lias and limestone suggests that it was an ornamental as well as utilitarian structure.

Walk back to the main road, turn right by the Tower House towards Bath until the houses end, then go through the gate on the left at the second of the two tracks coming down from the hill. The hedges soon end but the track is clear, winding across the field and going gently up the contours. Keep the belt of trees above you. Below, you get another view of Kelston Park. After a farm the path stays in the field along the bottom fence, with a big rabbit warren in the hedge to your left at the top of the field. Cross the stile onto the track and when you reach the second farm you join the Cotswold Way. Take it, climbing steeply.

The next half-mile has been spoilt, though the views are fine, with William Beckford's Lansdown Tower, built in the 1820s purely for sybaritic luxury and ostentation, prominent on the eastern skyline. You walk between barbed wire and share the Way with horses, but at least this will show you what roads were like in the 18th century, even to the extent of its periodic mud.

The Cotswold Way skirts Kelston Round Hill with its clump of trees; it loses the horses here and looks like a path again, marked with a white circle in a yellow arrow. Cross a track and keep climbing with wider and wider views and the crack of clay pigeon shooting in your ears until you reach Prospect Stile and the welcome level ground of Lansdown Racecourse, site of a Civil War battle. Keep left along the edge of the hill until the ditch and rampart of an Iron Age hill-fort bar the way. Walk to the right in its ditch to get a good impression of its strength then cut in left over the rampart to cross the wide enclosure. No one would live permanently in this dry, windy place; it was only intended as a refuge for people and their animals in times of danger. When you come to the original, well-preserved entrance gap you look down at North Stoke church and can see what must have been the Celtic village site on a high, but sheltered, shoulder of the hill. The path leads straight down over one stile, then bears right to another a few yards right of the church.

Now you are on a lane with a remarkable series of buildings ahead of you in this small isolated hamlet. But a word of warning before we begin – North Stoke has been seriously damaged since the first edition of this book by a rash of plastic-framed windows. Fortunately the first farm by the church has kept its original cross-mullioned windows with bulging 'bolection' surrounds. It has two ponds – a square one for ducks and a round one for geese. St Martin's tower is unusual as you can date it by an inscription. It was built in 1735 of robust squared masonry unlike the rest of the church which is of coursed rubble. Walk up the path to the porch to see the date-stone. As a note in the church records, St Martin's is "kept open by the efforts of forty or so adults who live around it", and is well worth a visit. There are charmingly naive wall monuments to the Ward family with curiously phonetic verses, an angular font which looks like an anvil and a fine old copy of a Correggio painting.

Back in the village street the cottages on the left have

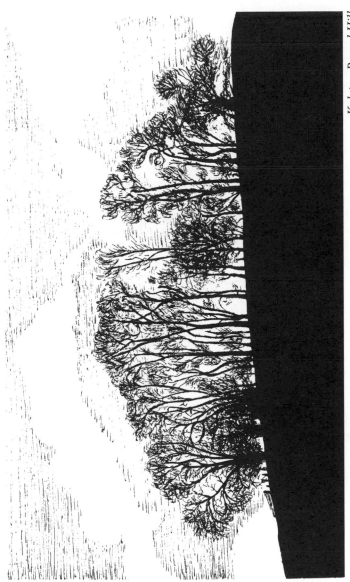

Kelston Round Hill

edge-moulded mullions so are early 18th-century. Manor Farm of about 1680 has ovolo-moulded mullions, continuous string courses and relieving arches over the windows and a good classical shell hood. But Manor House Farm, though not much older, is in gabled Cotswold traditional. Its original casements have been replaced by modern plastic windows. And from here onwards you can trace the steps of the plastic window salesman as he blights almost every house. After the bend in the street there is a row of early 20th-century Arts and Crafts cottages with a round carriage arch built around the older Rose Cottage. Opposite this interesting group is Sandygates, a riotous bungalow with post box, street sign (did the owners bring it from their last street?) and even a bus stop. With a last early Victorian Gothic house on your right the lane pitches headlong down to the main road.

Turn right here for 75 yards to a public footpath on your left with a broken stile and a notice: "NO FISHING". Ahead are two strange truncated grey pyramids and a huddle of dusty grey houses. This is Kelston Mill and the pyramids were the annealing ovens of a brass foundry. William Champion, who produced zinc and the pewter-like 'spelter', built these around 1760.

The tall row of workers' cottages is a remarkable survival with its range of wash-boiler chimneys for the back kitchens. Walk along the front of the houses to the stile and follow the path along the riverside until you come to the bridge of heavy steel girders. This carried the old railway line from Mangotsfield to Green Park station in Bath, now converted into Sainsbury's. The line is now the Avon Walkway but we only follow it for 100 yards to the left until it crosses our next track on a stone bridge.

There are steps down and the track, clearly marked, heads north-east through open fields to Kelston. Fork right at the little stream towards the Tower House. Three stiles bring you to a farm. The gate between this farm and the thatched house leads to the village lane. Pause at the bend to look at the Old School House, built in 1863 for children and now in 1998 a luxury hotel for cats. The lane leads you to Kelston church where we began, but if you need refreshment before you go home, The Old Crown just on the main road is welcoming.

Doynton, Dyrham and a hill walk on the west-facing Cotswolds

Length: 5 miles/Grade B

Map: O.S. Explorer 155 (Bristol & Bath)

Theme: From workaday Doynton to debonair Dyrham – a contrast in village styles, with a splendid walk back from a stately home in a sealed-off valley through the wreck of Celtic field systems.

Transport: By car – out of Bath up Lansdown Hill on the road north-west to Wick. Cross the A420 to Doynton, one mile further, and park in the road opposite the church (ST 720251).
By bus – Ryan's Coaches (No. 729, Fridays and Saturdays; tel: 01225 424157) operate a limited service to Doynton church.

Dyrham Park: The main entrance for cars is on the A46, but walkers approaching the house from the village can buy tickets at the door. Admission to the house: adults £5.40, children £2.70 (1998). Open 3 April to 1 November, 12.00-5.30, except Wednesdays and Thursdays.

Things to look out for:
1 Three combes with varied fortunes
2 The gabled roofline of a 'Linda Hall' house
3 Hatchments
4 Two houses stuck together by a third
5 A river god without water
6 Foxes and pheasants
7 Mediaeval encaustic tiles

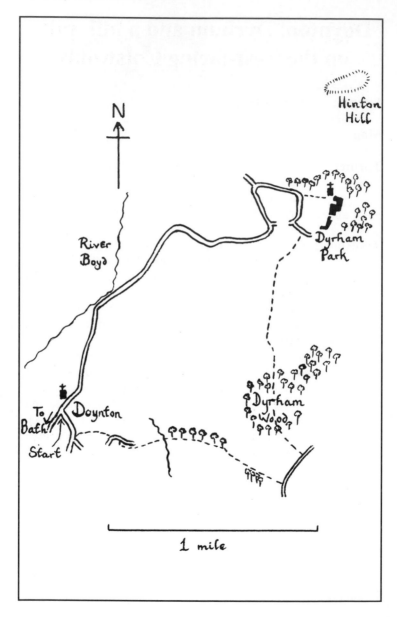

N

Hinton
Hill

River
Boyd

Dyrham
Park

Dyrham
Wood

To
Bath

Doynton

Start

1 mile

Itinerary

Unless you pay to enter Dyrham Park and eat in the Orangery, the only place on this walk where you will get refreshment is The Cross House on the High Street at Doynton. This serves a good range of pub food. Aside from Dyrham House, there is more interesting domestic architecture in Doynton than in its aristocratic neighbour, so spend a little time before you leave the village – don't miss Purbeck and Roselands cottages near the pub. Holy Trinity deserves a look for its herringbone masonry, Saxo-Norman in date. In the churchyard there are lots of fine 18th-century chest tombs and one amazing headstone to Edward and Hannah Nicholls with symbols of death and destruction in crisp carving. Inside the only interest is the curious uncut capitals of the aisle arcade: the money must have run out when the church was restored in 1864.

On your left as you walk through the village is Court Barton, a complex of new houses around an old barn which has been sensitively converted. I will leave it to you to decide whether the new classical columns are appropriate. Look out for the charming datestone (EGM 1721) on the cottages opposite. As you leave the village, going north on the Dyrham lane, you pass Court Farm, a lovely homespun straggle of 17th- and early 18th-century vernacular building, with just one rather bewildered classical pediment applied to its entrance front by an owner who wanted 'to do a Dyrham'. Pause by the garden gate and enjoy the enormous Wellingtonia towering up above you. Your last village visual is the hideously converted Old Chapel with ruinous strap pointing to its walls and garish plastic-frame windows and dormers.

Continue walking on this lane where the River Boyd keeps you company for a while and so sometimes do foxes. As the road swings round to Dyrham you get a remarkable Celtic Britain view with the ramparts of Hinton hill-fort ahead and a whole range of strip lynchets (ridges for cultivation on a hillside) terracing the Cotswold slopes to your right. Don't turn directly right into Dyrham village at the junction but take the Pucklechurch road for a few hundred yards, then turn right and sneak in the more interesting and leafy back way by The Old Rectory to the church.

You will remember St Peter's most for its extraordinary position, squeezed between a steep wood and the rich limestone cliffs of Dyrham House. The church connects with the great house and you get wonderful glimpses of the west front and the remains of the late 17th-century Dutch-style formal water gardens from the churchyard. Inside the church are nine funeral hatchments and in the south aisle, with its its beautiful encaustic tiles on the floor, are the enjoyably vulgar monuments of the Wynter Blathwayts who built the house. The west front was designed by the Hugenot, Samuel Hauduroy in 1694 – the balcony is quite un-English. The stables next to it are probably by Edward Wilcox, general foreman of the more famous architect William Talman, who liked to copy bits of continental architecture he had seen in prints. You can get an uninterrupted view of this whole façade through the fine gates in the lane leading on to the village. The National Trust likes people to enter by car from the main road a mile away and that certainly provides a surprise view of the totally different east front designed by Talman in 1698 which looks like a Genoese palace.

To reach the house take the track up to your left by the disused Gothick lodge, turn left at the top and walk down to the stable court. From here you get an even more surprising sideways view of the two separate bits of the house stuck together by the hall of the earlier, Tudor manor. The sound of water hurrying underground at this point is very atmospheric. The spring once began as a cascade in the park with, at its head, a statue of Neptune. If you look to the horizon you can still see the river god but he is now in a sea of grass. You should probably pay the entrance fee to the house as there is much to enjoy: walls of stamped Spanish leather and a Murillo next to its Gainsborough copy.

Tomb at St Peter's Church, Dyrham

But the real excitement is the exterior – the way in which its complex of golden stone façades shuts off a deep Cotswold combe into a secret world of aristocratic pleasure.

Now go back to the Gothick lodge, turn left and then left again up the hill. Above you is the gabled roofline of Poplar Lodge, one of those local yeoman's houses often called a 'Linda Hall' house after the woman who wrote a book about them. Part way up the hill is a footpath to the right (The Cotswold Way) signposted "Pennsylvania 2km, Cold Ashton 3km". Take this and you will soon reach two more combes that have developed quite differently to the Dyrham valley. In the first, with lynchets all around it, is Sands Farm. It is a matter of opinion whether the terraces are mediaeval or celtic, but the soft, sandy soil with frequent springs and sheltered areas has attracted settlers from the very earliest times. *Deorham*, the battle when the Saxons separated the Celts of Wales from the Celts of the south-western peninsular, was fought here in 577.

The last combe is the loneliest, its lynchets are almost ploughed out and a wood broods over it. Cross the bridge and stile, keep the wood on your left before entering it at the gate. Most woods have a charm but this one's is ruinous. Its trees were felled years ago and all the growth is secondary from the old stumps. You climb up a dry water course into a field and for 300 yards follow a busy, dangerous road, but your way back downhill again is through the gate in the first field to the right.

There is a wide view over Vale and Severn but now you will need to go carefully, with your eye on the tower of Doynton church far below you. The right of way leads almost straight down the steep, occasionally marshy fields towards this tower. Keep the copse on the edge of the escarpment to your left across the first large field. Cross a stile and make for the bottom right-hand corner of the next field. Three sturdy stiles lead you to a wide gateway where, beside some waterworks, there is a post with three yellow arrows pointing, one to the left, one where you have been and the other forward where you must go, still keeping the hedge on your right.

The path continues over two more stiles as the ground levels out, with the second built around an old plough. You cross a track here and two more fields bring you out where Watery Lane meets Toghill Lane. Nip left a few yards up the lane to see Old Brewery House, an early 18th-century Bath-style house with a two-slope mansard roof; the thick glazing bars of its sash windows give away the early date. Then make for the village and the two large houses on your left and right which provide interesting contrasts. First on the right is Rectory Farmhouse in the native Cotswold tradition – all cross-mullioned windows and gabled dormers. The Old Rectory on the left has abandoned this homely vernacular and gone politely classical with a pedimented doorcase, sash windows and a double-span roof for a spacious attic. The sombre, evergreen planting of yews, firs and laurel in the garden is perfect for a rectory.

A very brief walk down the lane and to the left is The Cross House, to the right is the church where you began. Before you leave look here for blocks of iridescent clinker that line the walls – by-products of the Bristol area's brass and copper smelting – and the boldly-lettered cast-iron bridge sign.

The Roman Road and St Catherine

Length: 6^1/$_2$ miles/Grade A

Map: O.S. Explorer 155 (Bristol & Bath)

Theme: A walk to introduce the Cotswolds in two contrasted moods – sweeping views from the high lonely fields and a sheltered valley patterned by history. There are no pubs on this walk so take a packed lunch and drink. If you are travelling by bus you can get refreshment when you finish the walk in Batheaston at the Northend inn.

Transport: By car – take the A4 London road to Batheaston (2^1/$_2$ miles). Fork left in the village uphill on the signposted road to Marshfield and Colerne. This is the Fosse Way. At the top of the hill, after two miles, park on the verge opposite the lodge to Southernwood (ST 798702)
By bus – The No. 228 service (not on Sundays) will drop you at the starting-point. Your route will end in Batheaston on the A4 with a frequent No. 13 or 13B service back to Bath.

Things to look out for:
1   The change in farmhouses 1680-1860
2   The way cottages are being restored
3   A leaping hare in stone
4   A rare Prior's window in St Catherine's church
5   Native trees and alien planting
6   Micro-climates and vegetation
7   Weekend ballooning, parachuting, light aircraft

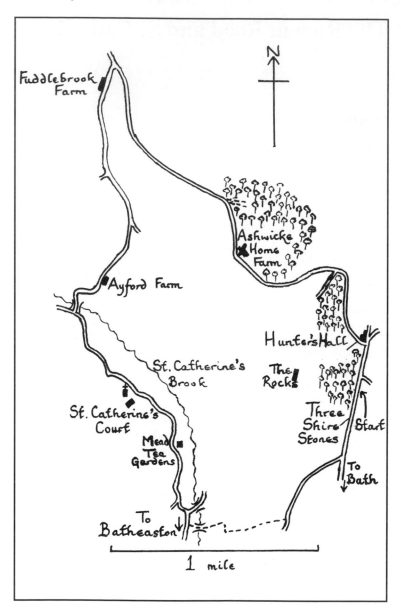

Itinerary

The first half mile is the only bit where you'll see much traffic but the views make up for it. Walk back to the Three Shire Stones at the end of the wall on your right. They mark the spot where Gloucestershire, Wiltshire and Somerset meet. They are in the form of a cromlech and were put up as a fake megalithic monument in 1859, probably to record the site of a chambered long barrow. Go down into the original fosse of the Roman road which is built up like a causeway above the fields on either side and enjoy the cathedral-like nave of beech trees which line the ditch. Now turn back and keep an eye on the walls as you set out on the walk. The art of laying them goes back thousands of years and different shapes of stone have names like quar, maverday, long wivett and middle batchelor.

Hidden in the park on your left is the ruin of a Victorian castle called The Rocks. You will get a dramatic view of it later. What you can't miss is Hunter's Hall, a big farm like a barracks at the crossroads where we go sharp left for Marshfield. The farm has chamfered mullioned windows but is perfectly symmetrical so must be an 18th-century remodelling of an earlier house. When it was built the farmer still housed his workforce under his own roof. The porch and the rough-pointed openings in the side wall of the farm buildings are fake Gothick of about 1800. So is the elegant wrought-iron sign-holder with its curvaceous quatrefoils. Nowadays, Cotswold farm buildings often get converted into houses and someone has been ingeniously at work here with the usual obtrusive hard-wood stained windows and doors.

Our lane runs along the top of a larch wood. Don't take Oakwood Lane downhill to the left. Further on, Ashwicke Home Farm on the right overlooks native oaks in a deep valley with the ruins of The Rocks commanding the view to your left. Some of the windows of the farm and its outbuildings have ovolo-moulded mullions – look for the one in the side wall of the gabled cottage by the road. These date the complex to the late 17th century. There is a distinct air of affluent grandeur to the farmyard.

The Cotswolds are famous for micro-climates. You will run into one round the next bend: a mini micro-climate with bushy ivy and common polypody ferns growing down in a sheltered dip. Over to your right, behind the imported conifers of an arboretum or tree garden, is Ashwicke Hall, another Victorian castle of 1857 with big towers corbelled out on their top storeys. At the next bend is the atmospheric, creeper-covered west lodge to the Hall. This has a separate pedestrian arch with beautiful leaf carving and a robust ironwork gate. Look up to spot the leaping hare on the gable end and the conifers and holm oaks that surround the little building.

After the lodge we come to Ashwicke Grange, all sharp angles like a bent elbow. This is another Victorian estate building in a style usually described as 'muscular'; it looks to me as if it is screaming. The next stretch of road until the sharp left turn into Ayford lane at the Fuddlebrook is like a scrap of Thomas Hardy's Wessex with bare fields of winter wheat. Fuddlebrook Farm is grim with four cell-like labourers' cottages. It illustrates the stage of social housing after *Hunter's Hall*.

Then comes the dramatic bit. The lane pitches down a miniature gorge of hart's-tongue ferns into a tangled patch of country straight out of *Cider With Rosie*. Ayford Farm has a barn above it with a beautiful roof of graded stone slates. The house seems mysteriously deserted. There is a marked path to St Catherine on this side of the river but you may keep drier on the road. Cross the bridge and turn left at the T-junction. I saw three hovering hawks on this stretch when I was revising the walk.

St Catherine's Court and church seem caught in a time warp. Walk to the church alongside the Regency kissing gate and decorative wrought-iron fence. The church entrance has grand Edwardian gatepiers and an imperial flight of steps. Although the church looks 15th-century, the tower was rebuilt in 1704 – look for the inscription on the south face. The church is kept open and welcoming – a great place to begin if you are new to church crawling. Use the information boards inside. The Blanchard monument is a Madame Tussaud's display of 1631 with skulls in the pediment and kneeling children below the parents. Not all the glass in the east window is 15th-century, only trust the kneeling Prior Cantlow who enlarged the church

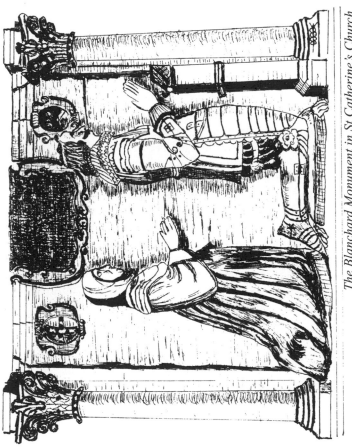

The Blanchard Monument in St Catherine's Church

in 1490. The polychromatic effect of the green tiles, mosaics and painted pulpit is all due to the Strutt family who lived at the Court. Their tragic history is touchingly commemorated by a cross the Germans placed on the Flanders grave of Richard Neville in 1915 and the Festival of Britain-style organ screen set up to two later brothers who died in the Second World War.

Walk up to the Strutt family enclosure in the churchyard to get the best view of the Court with its columned porch and canted oriel window above. The house has a Tudor core but was made more impressive in the early 17th century and given the opulent Edwardian treatment in the late 19th century. Beautiful terraced gardens with steps, balustrades extending up the hillside to the west are another part of this romantic remodelling.

The lonely part of the walk is over now. High up on your left you will see the ruins of The Rocks in the woods, converted cottages are strung out along the road and, if you are catching the bus you continue down the lane to Batheaston. If you came by car you have a stiff climb ahead. After Oakford Lane comes in on the left, take the first marked Public Path, also on the left. Go straight downhill, over the bridge, and up the hill on pebbled cart ruts which can be muddy. Over a stile to your right, the path goes on up between two hedges, pretty steep and, therefore, usually dry. When you reach the lane, turn left for a third of a mile. Left at the main road will return you to your car.

Castle Farm and a Marshfield Town Walk

Length:　2 miles/Grade C

Map:　O.S. Explorer 155 (Bristol & Bath)

Theme:　How to read an old town like a book – the English equivalent of a Wild West ghost town that boomed in the first half of the 18th century through the coaching trade and malting, then went dead on its cold Cotswold ridge until cars brought in the commuters. This walk has more pubs than miles.

Transport:　By car – 10 miles from Bath, east out on the A4, left on the A46, then right along the A420. This was the old coach road from Bristol to London and one reason for Marshfield's prosperity. When you approach the town take the lane left to Castle Farm ($\frac{1}{2}$ mile). You can't miss this with its show of towers. Park on a wide verge anywhere near. (ST 772745) By bus – there is a very limited service either with Ryan's Coaches (No.729 on Fridays and Saturdays; tel: 01225 424157) or Andrew's Coaches (No. 79 on Wednesdays; tel: 01225 891404) and return is impossible the same day so it is better to go by car.

Things to look out for:
1　The Bloody Cranesbill flowers on the verges in summer
2　Crown glass and how to date a house by its windows
3　A church killed by caring
4　Burgage plots and mediaeval back gardens
5　The oldest loo in England?
6　The Cotswolds coping with commuter housing
7　Where Dylan Thomas was suspected of being a German spy

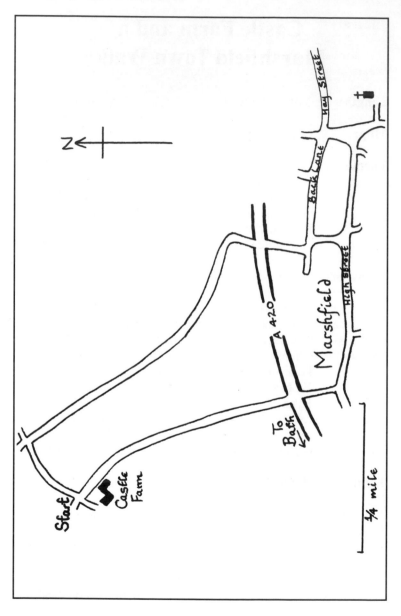

Itinerary

At Castle Farm nothing is quite what it seems. Through the farmyard at the back is a surviving 16th-century long house where farmer and cattle once lived under one roof. The towers, battlements and lancet windows of the farmhouse are all mock Gothic of the 1790s, built for the estate steward by the Codrington family of Dodington Park. Although the mansion is quite far away on the other side of the M4, the Codringtons owned most of Marshfield and had the farm tricked out like a castle to liven up this lonely spot. The tall firs add to the Romantic gloom of the place. Take a look at the staddle stones and real Gothic church finials before you set off. The fields look bare and beautiful, a haven for larks, but this was probably the original site of Marshfield. It is called Westend Town. Mediaeval pottery and Roman tiles have been found here but the town moved south-east to control the road when roads began to mean money.

Walk to the crossroads and turn right. There used to be stones here to mark where King Oswald was supposedly crucified by the Mercians after the battle of *Marchfield* – the old fair was held at Marshfield on St Oswald's day. Turn right again back to the bypass, cross it and you are into an interesting new suburbia. See what you think of the first newish houses. They are made of reconstructed stone blocks and have concrete roof tiles with two humps that are called double Roman. Their man-made materials will never have the weathered colour and texture of natural stone.

Walk through the estate and cross Back Lane into Touching End Lane. It is not easy to add to an old town but at the junction is a genuine oldster – The Poplars. It has a gambrel, or mansard, double-slope roof of beautifully graded stone slates and the roadside front is of humble rubble masonry. But round the back is the show front of colour-washed render lined out to look like a smooth squared finish of stone blocks called ashlar. This true ashlar facing can be seen all over Marshfield as local people picked up the fine masonry fashions from Bath in the early 18th century. This particular house got stuck half way to being modern. The round-headed window in the centre is 18th-century but the side windows with their upright stone bars or mullions are still in the old style Cotswold vernacular.

As you walk on left along Back Lane you are into a mediaeval street plan. On your left are the new houses trying to fit in, some of them doing very well because they use real stone: my favourite cast-iron house sign is Yeoman's Retreat. On your right are the burgage plots perfectly preserved and still used for their proper purposes. These were back gardens and work areas for the houses in the High Street. On the south side of that street are more plots and another back lane keeping the High Street free from carts. Like a French village, Marshfield has farms clustered along the street rather than scattered out on the windy hills. The next village was not called Cold Ashton for nothing so wrap up if you do this walk in winter.

Walk along Back Lane to Hay Street and on the right, just before the new houses begin, is Tythe Court. This was originally the manorial tithe barn and it has been converted into housing. Fortunately the carved stone corbels on the gable end have survived the conversion, but I find the brown-stained hardwood window frames and part-glazed doors particularly offensive. Across the road Nos. 19 and 20 have caught the 18th-century Bath fashion for ashlar fronts and neat Palladian-style pediments over the doors. No. 20 has modern plastic windows but upstairs number 19 has kept not only the original wooden sash windows, but also the beautiful textured crown glass with its greenish tints. Move your head to catch its roughness in the light.

Walk back and make for the church. The main building of the Lord Nelson on the left has lost its inn sign but kept the metal holder, and there is more crown glass. There is a beautiful shell hood to the doorway which has a bulging surround called a bolection moulding – a sure sign of an early 18th-century date. The pub has a restaurant and accommodation. Turn left into Market Place and walk down to the grand house on the right which was the vicarage until recently. It was refronted in 1730 with a pediment and chunky, recessed segmental-headed windows in a style that seems more baroque than Bath classical. There are earlier, 17th-century cross-mullioned windows and gabled pitching eyes for hay in the stable block to the side.

Castle Farm, Marshfield

The church is usually open and beautifully kept, but in 1860 the Victorians scraped it clean of plaster and there is little of interest. But look out for the benefaction boards in the children's corner, the 17th-century altar table used now for a flower stand and the pitch-pine pews with their numbered doors. It is worth walking round the churchyard for the mystery of two large farmhouses in one farmyard. Perhaps two brothers inherited the manor equally.

Back towards the High Street is the old market place where the King William mummers play is performed on Boxing Day. Now almost every house for half a mile is interesting. Remember: the thicker the glazing bars and the more small panes of glass the older the house. The Catherine Wheel pub has 32-pane sashes so it is early, about 1700. Here there is another fine shell hood and bulging bolection surrounds to the window frames. This front is another up-dating of an earlier house which can be seen around the back. The Tolsey Hall next door was the town hall when Marshfield was a bustling borough. It was first built in 1690 so you could say the Public Conveniences downstairs are about 300 years old.

Further down the street on the left is No. 83 which deserves attention. It has 12-pane sashes with thin glazing bars so it is late 18th-century, probably about 1790 with slick, Adam-style columns to its porch. On either side are two small carriage entrances with paper thin pediments; the one to the left has been filled in. Not many houses in Marshfield are this late because after 1750 the Bristol-London traffic tended to pass through Bath and the town began to dwindle. But there were still eight maltings and a brewery in 1870. A little further back on the right is The Malting House where the poet Dylan Thomas stayed in 1940. One of his gang of young men was called Glock so the locals suspected they were Germans spying on airfields.

At the end of the village there is a charming range of eight Almshouses, originally founded in 1619 and rebuilt in the 19th century with a clock tower and spire. Take George Lane, the path by the side of the almshouses, cross the bypass again and walk back through instant loneliness to Castle Farm.

Badminton Park
and a grand ducal progress

Length: 10 miles/Grade A

Maps: O.S. Explorer 168 (Stroud, Tetbury & Malmesbury)

Theme: This is not a walk for picturesque views. It crosses the wide, open Cotswold uplands where oak trees are as stunted now as when Canaletto painted them. But it is designed to make the term 'ducal' mean something. It introduces an historic estate in full working order and an area of country – Beaufortshire – which has changed less since 1800 than any similar part of Britain.

Transport: By car – north out of Bath on the A46. Cross the M4, turn right at Old Sodbury for Malmesbury. Notice the charming Gothic lodge to Lyegrove House, then take the first left at the clump of holm oaks for Badminton. As you enter the village turn left at a thatched cottage that looks like a creeping hedgehog and park your car (ST 805827).
By bus – there is no direct bus service from Bath to Badminton so this walk is strictly for motorists.

Things to look out for:
1 The park buildings of Thomas Wright and
2 The yew trees and holm oaks he often planted
3 Some famous jumps in the Badminton Horse Trials
4 A chambered prehistoric burial mound, neglected and open to the sky
5 The horse girls (but you'll need to make an early start)
6 One of the ten most beautiful small buildings in Britain
7 A ducal air strip

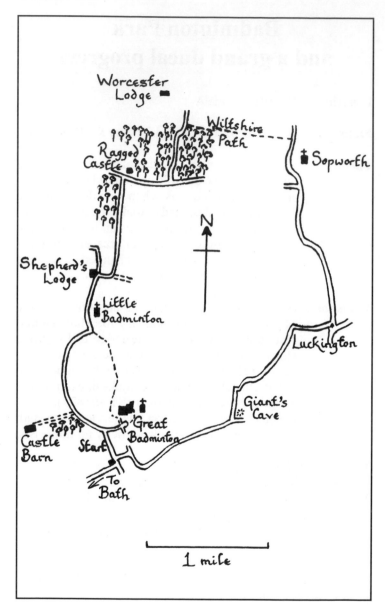

Itinerary

The architect and cosmology expert, Thomas Wright, designed many buildings for the 4th Duke of Beaufort between 1748 and 1752. Badminton has none of the natural advantages of a typical landscape park like lakes and valleys, so it needed broad belts of beech trees and fanciful buildings to define its limits. The cottage where the walk begins is the first of these, one of the earliest *ombrellos* or *cottages ornées* in the country. You are on Station Road, so called because the Victorian Duke of Beaufort would not allow the Great Western Railway to drive a tunnel through his land unless they built him a private station where trains had to stop on his command. Walk into the village with the playing fields on your right. Great Badminton has hardly an ugly house, all are in lovely faded earth colours – washed yellows and pale ochres, the Beaufort estate livery. Turn right at the cross-roads and note the contrast between the early 18th-century houses with their cross-mullions and leaded panes to your left and the range across the street with its Gothick touches and fancy bargeboards. Down the street on the right is a fine 1714 range of Almshouses with coronets, the Beaufort portcullis and the Beaufort beasts supporting the cartouches – see if you can spot the chains.

It is a must to go through the gates marked "Strictly Private" (to cars only) to see the parish church because, although this is usually locked, you get fascinating views of the vast lumbering ducal mansion to which it is physically attached. It is like going to one of the great Polish or Czech Republic estates before the First World War. William Kent's cupolas rise up on the north front and there is an elegant formal garden to the south. In the churchyard is the simple gravestone to the present Duke's wife, Lady Caroline. As you walk back to the gates look through the stable arch to see the yard where the veterinary inspections take place before the cross-country section of the famous Trials begins.

Retrace your steps to the street and take the road to your right which is a legitimate footpath and leads you through the richly-textured estate buildings. In the morning it is alive with happy young women exercising horses. On the left are the kennels of the Beaufort Hunt and, if you look over the wall here, there is a rustic grotto arch for the private path linking the house to the hounds. The handsome octagonal house on the left is the Kennels Lodge. One great interest of the park is that so many lodges of the various ducal servants survive.

You can walk across the park here, there is a right of way, but if you want to see the western park buildings go back into the village and carry straight on at the junction towards Little Badminton. You will soon pass under an arch of one of the many far-flung drives. At the end of the wood down a farm track on the left is Thomas Wright's atmospheric Castle Barn, built as an eyecatcher to be seen across the fields and originally painted red and white. There is no right of way to the barn so enjoy views of it as you walk to the next lodges. The first is the upper Slait Lodge with miniature turrets at the corners. Between this and the lower lodge to your right you can see some of the cross-country jumps of the Horse Trials. Bounding the horizons beyond the airstrip are the majestic beech belts which old Queen Mary made it her wartime task to trim and clear – naturally she never finished.

Little Badminton is out of Goldsmith's *Deserted Village* rather than Hardy's Dorset. If you crossed the park you will have come out on the public road at the lodge here, and it is worth making a brief circuit of the place to appreciate its faded charm of barns, church, dovecote and unaltered cottages. Back on the lane you can see across the fields to your left Swangrove, an enchanting pleasure pavilion built by the 2nd Duke for his mistress. Turn right at the Shepherd's Lodge, keep to the public road and, as you follow the mile-long straight, you will notice on your left the formal avenues of the 17th-century estate. At the end of the straight you will see a tell-tale clump of yews and holly. Hidden in this greenery is Wright's weirdest folly, The Ragged Castle, still largely intact with rock-faced masonry and frowning battlements. Turn right across the three-mile drive from the house to Worcester Lodge, then left through the thick Bullpark Wood.

As you emerge from the trees you can see William Kent's masterpiece, the Worcester Lodge, across the park to the left – it takes its name from the courtesy title of the Duke's heir, the

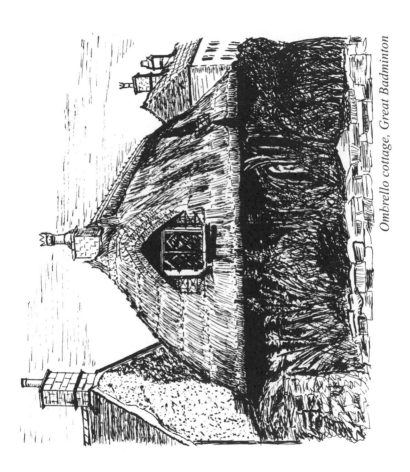

Ombrello cottage, Great Badminton

Marquis of Worcester. The Lodge has a superb variety of profile and dominates the axis you have just crossed. The central room on the first floor has rich plasterwork and was used in the 18th century as a ducal dining pavilion. Nowadays the Beaufort Hunt meets here for its stirrup cup on Boxing Day. Go through the gateway on the right-hand side of the road and follow the edge of the wood. When it ends follow the path left and then right beside the next vast field. This track is known as The Wiltshire Path and keeps the hedge on its right until it reaches Sopworth.

Now the walk turns right and heads south. Sopworth and the next village, Luckington, are shuttered stone places of some charm. In neither is the church of much consequence, but each has a few good early 18th-century cross-mullioned houses and at Luckington the Old Royal Ship pub may be just what you need at this stage of a Grade A walk.

Take Cherry Orchard Lane out of Luckington, bend left at the first barn and continue another mile to the Giant's Cave. This is on your left under scrubby growth just before the T-junction – a large prehistoric burial place which deserves restoration. You can scramble over the stone slabs which once lined its passages and even make out the chamber entrance. The lane to the right is Luckington Lane and features as one of the hardest jumps in the Badminton Horse Trials, just how testing you will be able to judge as it actually crosses the road.

As you head for Badminton, the east front of the house appears on your right and you are soon back in the village having circled Beaufortshire. But be warned, there is no ducal pub! Badminton is as dry as the limestone on which it lies.

Country Code

Guard against all risk of fire
Every year costly damage is done by fire to crops, plantations, woodlands and heath. Picnic fires not properly put out are one cause. A cigarette thrown away or a pipe knocked out can start a raging inferno. Be careful – a spark may do terrible damage and destroy a lifetime's work.

Fasten all gates
Animals, if they stray, can do great damage to crops and to themselves. Wandering animals are a menace to themselves and others on country roads. Even if you find a gate open, always shut it behind you.

Keep your dogs under close control
It is natural for a dog to chase anything that will run. Keep your dog out of temptation's way. Animals are easily frightened and the chasing of a ewe or cow may result in loss of young. When near animals or walking along the road, keep your dog on a lead.

Keep to public paths across farmland
Crops are damaged by treading, at any stage of growth. Patches of flattened corn make it difficult to harvest. Grass is also a valuable crop, remember. So please walk in single file where a path crosses a field. This keeps the path well defined and saves the crop on either side.

Use gates and stiles to cross fences, hedges and walls
If you force your way through a fence or hedge, you will weaken it. Where a person has gone an animal may follow. Stones dislodged from walls may injure people and animals, and damage crops and machinery.

Take your litter home
All litter is unsightly. Broken glass, tins and plastic bags are dangerous. they may also damage costly machinery and hold up work which it is vital to finish while the weather lasts. So leave no litter or picnic remains.

Help to keep all water clean
Water is precious in the country. Never wash dishes or bathe in somebody's water supply or foul it in any other way, or interfere with water-troughs set for cattle.

Protect wildlife, plants and trees
Wild flowers give more pleasure to more people if left to grow. Plants should never be uprooted. Trees are valuable as well as beautiful: if they are damaged their health and beauty are harmed. Birds and their eggs, animals, plants and trees should be left alone.

Take special care on country roads
Drive carefully. Blind corners, hump-backed bridges, slow-moving farm machinery and led or driven animals are all hazards for the motorist. Walk carefully, too. It is generally safer to walk on the right, facing oncoming traffic.

Respect the life of the countryside
The life of the country centres on its work. While you are there, try to fit in. Country people have to leave their belongings in the open, roads and paths run through their places of work, and you are on trust. Their work often involves hard labour. They keep early hours. So make as little noise as possible when you pass through villages in the evening. Be considerate, leave things alone, and so repay the local people for the pleasure their countryside has give you.